NORTH AMERICAN F-86 SABRE

The development of the jet engine represented a seminal period in the history of aviation, but it took many years to mature into a truly viable means of propulsion. An astonishing number of relatively primitive jet-powered aircraft emerged in the years that immediately followed World War Two, but despite the remarkable potential of the gas turbine, it resulted in the creation of some aircraft that were arguably no better than the propeller types that they were supposedly replacing. But there was one exception, in the shape of North American Aviation's F-86 Sabre. Although it was a relatively simple machine, powered by an equally unsophisticated jet engine, it embraced a completely new design concept – the swept wing. It first emerged as a rather disappointing naval fighter design with a fat, stubby fuselage and a conventional straight wing. But when the aircraft was redesigned to incorporate a swept wing it became a completely different fighting machine, with a top speed and a rate of climb that few other aircraft could match. But even this achievement would not have been enough to ensure the Sabre's place in history. It was the Korean War that secured the Sabre's legendary status, providing the United States with a machine that could take on the mighty MiG-15 and win. The Sabre was a classic example of the right design at precisely the right time. Following the Korean War, the Sabre spread its wings around the world, becoming the 'standard' fighter-bomber for many countries, throughout the 1950s and 1960s. Ultimately, a staggering 9,860 Sabres were manufactured, and although the aircraft was retired from operational use many years ago, it can still be seen in civilian hands, thrilling airshow crowds across the globe, reminding spectators that the Sabre was something special – arguably the first 'real' jet fighter.

Tim McLelland (1962-2015)

In this second edition of the *Aeroplane Icons* series, we take a look at the story of the Sabre, and although space prohibits a thorough examination of every aspect of this aircraft's very full history, the following pages present a comprehensive celebration of a true legend.

Ben Dunnell

CONTENTS

(Photo: David Whitworth)

Cover photo: Darren Harbar

ISBN: 978 1 83632 046 3
Editor: Tim McLelland (1962-2015)
Updates/corrections, this edition: Paul Hamblin and Ben Dunnell
Senior editor, specials: Roger Mortimer
Email: roger.mortimer@keypublishing.com
Cover Design: Steve Donovan
Design: Paul Silk and SJmagic DESIGN SERVICES, India
Advertising Sales Manager: Sam Clark
Email: sam.clark@keypublishing.com
Tel: 01780 755131
Advertising Production: Becky Antoniades
Email: Rebecca.antoniades@keypublishing.com

SUBSCRIPTION/MAIL ORDER
Key Publishing Ltd, PO Box 300, Stamford, Lincs, PE9 1NA
Tel: 01780 480404
Subscriptions email: subs@keypublishing.com

Mail Order email: orders@keypublishing.com
Website: www.keypublishing.com/shop

PUBLISHING
Group CEO and Publisher: Adrian Cox

Published by
Key Publishing Ltd, PO Box 100, Stamford, Lincs, PE9 1XQ
Tel: 01780 755131 **Website:** www.keypublishing.com

PRINTING
Precision Colour Printing Ltd, Haldane, Halesfield 1, Telford, Shropshire. TF7 4QQ

DISTRIBUTION
Seymour Distribution Ltd, 2 Poultry Avenue, London, EC1A 9PU
Enquiries Line: 02074 294000.

NAUTICAL FURY

The United States Navy's new Jet captures the interest of the US Army Air Forces, and the Sabre is born.

A trio of FJ-1 Fury fighters from the Oakland Naval Air Reserve pictured high over San Francisco during 1950. *(Photo: US Navy)*

Although the F-86 Sabre is probably best known as a key participant in the Korean War, the origins of its design can be traced back to World War Two, when North American Aviation (NAA) first proposed a jet-powered fighter for the United States Navy, capable of supporting the planned invasion of Japan that was expected to take place in May 1946. Of course the jet engine was still a relatively new concept at that time, and the US Navy was reluctant to invest too much support in just this single project. Instead, it looked at a variety of competing designs that were proposed by various manufacturers, resulting in some well-known early jets such as the XF6U-1 Pirate and more exotic designs such as Ryan's FR-1 Fireball. North American's project, the NA-134, was drawn up in 1944 and three prototypes were ordered for the US Navy on 1 January 1945. The XFJ-1 was a simple and unimaginative design with straight wings and a single General Electric J35 jet engine, fed by an intake that ran from the nose under the cockpit. On 28 May an order was placed for 100 production aircraft, now designated by North American Aviation as the NA-141. While production of the Navy's fighter got under way, North American's designers turned their attention to an emerging requirement from the United States Army Air Forces (AAF) for a new day fighter, capable of performing escort fighter missions and medium-range fighter-bomber tasks. No specific performance requirements were stipulated, other than a top speed of at least 600 mph. NAA proposed a derivative of its NA-141, tailored to the needs of the AAF and this design, the NA-140, led to an order (placed on 18 May 1945) for three prototypes, designated as the XP-86. At that time the AAF still referred to fighters as 'Pursuit' aircraft.

The FJ-1 Fury was the aircraft from which the F-86 Sabre was derived. Although visibly simple in terms of design, it became a remarkably fast and agile machine, when its straight wings were replaced by a new swept-angle design. ***(Photo: US Navy)***

The two designs were expected to be largely similar, but as the details of specific Air Force and Navy requirements were examined more carefully, changes were made to both aircraft that were more than superficial. They retained the same J35 engine and the same armament (three 0.50 calibre machine guns mounted on each side of the aircraft's forward fuselage), but the naval type had to be modified to incorporate a stronger airframe structure with tougher landing gear, designed to withstand the stresses of carrier operations. In stark contrast, the Air Force's aircraft incorporated a slimmer and lighter fuselage, together with a thinner wing to provide the performance

The bulky proportions of the FJ-1's fuselage are emphasised by this view of the aircraft in storage configuration, the nose wheel replaced by a temporary 'Jockey wheel' that enabled the aircraft to be stacked in a tail-high attitude inside carrier hangars, without any need for wing folding. ***(Photo: US Navy)***

◄

The Fury's wing span was designed to fit within the parameters of the US Navy's carrier deck lifts. From this angle, the origins of the F-86 Sabre's design are very clear. *(Photo: US Navy)*

►

This Fury from VF-5 ran off the runway at NAS North Island during 1959, resulting in extensive damage to the aircraft's nose and undercarriage. It is believed that it was written off. *(Photo: US Navy)*

The unremarkable FJ-1 Fury (pictured here at Los Alamitos) made the US Navy's first operational jet landing at sea, paving the way for the Navy's future carrier power. The Fury was capable of launching from carriers without catapult assistance, but the aircraft's initial low speed and acceleration made such launches potentially dangerous. *(Photo: US Navy)*

The XP-86 prototype (45-9587) made its first flight on 1 October 1947. Photographs of the first take-off are few, possibly because photographers at Muroc appear to have misjudged the considerable length of the XP-86's take-off run. These rare images show the aircraft at the beginning of its first and second flights, and during the maiden flight when the aircraft was first exhibiting gear retraction problems. ***(Photos: USAF)***

that the AAF had stipulated. A 10% thickness-to-chord ratio was employed on the XP-86 wing but even with this superior version of the naval design, it was estimated that the XP-86 would still fail to achieve the 600mph top speed that had been requested. With a gross weight of 11,500lb and a maximum speed of 525mph at 10,000ft, the aircraft's combat radius was estimated at 297 miles (with a 170-gallon drop tank under each wing). The AAF approved the manufacture of a mock-up for further investigation, but it was clear to both NAA and the AAF that the XP-86 was likely to be a disappointment if it proceeded in its current form. In fact, it would be inferior to the Republic XP-84 Thunderjet that was nearing completion. North American's designers studied the project extensively and concluded that even with further improvements, the straight-wing layout would never be capable of reaching speeds of 600mph or more. The only practical way of meeting this speed capability would be to embrace a swept-wing design, although contemporary thinking on this subject suggested that such a radical proposal would result in all manner of associated problems such as low-speed instability and wing tip stall. The concept of swept-wing design was already understood and had been pursued by German designers with some demonstrable success. A swept-wing reduced airflow drag and reduced compressibility effects, enabling aircraft to achieve much greater speeds. Germany had already produced the remarkable Me 262 jet fighter and the formidable Me 163 Komet interceptor, which incorporated a 15-degree swept-wing and a rocket engine that gave the aircraft a top speed of approximately 600mph – the very figure that the AAF was seeking. Most importantly, the German designers had solved the risks of low-speed instability by incorporating leading-edge slats into the Komet's wing design. These extended automatically at low speed and increased the aircraft's wing chord, thereby increasing lift. The wing slat concept had originally been developed by Handley Page in Britain some years previously, but its effectiveness had not been demonstrated with any clarity until the Komet appeared. North American's design team laboriously translated countless German research documents that had been recovered by the United States, and a complete Me 262 A wing was given to the company so that its leading-edge slat design could be examined in detail. North American's designers agreed that if wing slats were incorporated into the design, a swept-wing could be adopted for the XP-86 and by the summer of 1945 NAA was investigating both straight-wing and swept-wing configurations, the latter being based on the proposed fully swept-wing derivative of the Me 262. During August of that year, NAA's aerodynamicist Larry Greene proposed that the swept-wing should be adopted and the design team (led by John Atwood and Chief Aerodynamicist Ed Horkey) took their proposal to the AAF for approval. On 18 August a Research and Development grant was agreed, enabling the swept-wing to be developed further and within a few weeks a wind tunnel model was being tested. Initial results were encouraging but a great deal of time was devoted to the issue of what aspect ration should be employed. The ratio of the wing's span and chord (width) had to be a compromise between two conflicting requirements. High aspect ratio would endow the aircraft with greater range, whereas a lower (broader) ratio would provide much better stability. The result was a ratio of 5.0, but further testing of a 6.0 wing (combined with the laminar profile that had been designed for the company's P-51 Mustang) demonstrated that it provided a much better lift-to-drag ratio. Combined with leading-edge slats that delivered satisfactory low-speed stability, this was the design that was initially proposed to the AAF. However, further wind tunnel testing revealed that despite the employment of numerous wing slat variations, the 6.0 aspect ratio wing suffered from a potentially lethal pitch-up tendency that would be unacceptable for a production combat aircraft. By March 1946 the earlier 5.0 aspect ratio wing was adopted and this was eventually refined to 4.79 with a sweep angle of 35 degrees, combined with a thickness-to-chord ratio of 11% at the wing root, decreasing to 10% at the wing tip. Evidence of airflow separation across the wing's trailing edge then resulted in an extension of some four inches across the entire span, but once this was incorporated into the design, the XP-86's wing shape was fixed. NAA's Chief Engineer Ray Rice advised the AAF that development of the swept-wing would delay the XP-86 programme by some months when compared to the Navy's XFJ-1, but the dramatic improvement in performance would make the delay worthwhile, and agreement was given on 1 November 1945 to proceed. A contract was issued on 20 December 1946 (AC-16013) for 33 production-standard P-86A aircraft, together with 190 P-86B machines, incorporating a slightly wider fuselage that was intended to accommodate larger undercarriage components. The contract was eventually changed to cover a further 188 P-86A aircraft (plus two P-86C Penetration Fighter prototypes) when improvements in landing gear design made the proposed wider fuselage modification unnecessary.

Most of the XP-86 airframe was manufactured conventionally, although new production processes had to be introduced for the wing. Because of the wing's extremely thin cross section, the traditional rib and stringer construction could not be employed and NAA's Dick Schleicker introduced the use of one-piece milling techniques, enabling the wing's structure to be formed from a solid billet, incorporating necessary vertical stiffeners across the span. A NAA report describes the design in more detail:

'A double skin structure with hat sections between layers extends from the centre section to the outboard edges of the outer panel fuel tanks, replacing the conventional rib and stringer construction in that region. Tapered skins have been used to save weight. The inboard upper skin, for example, is .250 inches thick at the wing root and .064 inches at the joint where it meets the outboard skin; the latter tapers from .064 inches at the joint to .032 inches at the wing tip. Specially equipped milling machines, using carbide-tipped fly cutters up to 12 inches in diameter, were set up in North American's main plant to solve the new fabrication problems presented by these skins. The most complicated skin, on which three operations are required to obtain compound tapers, is completely machined in only 45 minutes. Use of 75S aluminum alloy throughout to provide a maximum strength-weight ratio has also complicated these production processes, as have extremely close tolerances required by both structural and aerodynamic considerations. As an example, a tolerance of only .002 inches is allowable on external rivet heads. This makes it necessary to shave about 15% off them after assembly. The need for maximum fuel space in the new thin structure has further complicated design. This requirement, heightened by the rapid increase in fuel consumption accompanying higher speeds, has been the factor chiefly responsible for the growth in size of fighter aircraft that has marked the post-War period. The XF-86 for example, is some 40% heavier than the F-51H'.

The wing leading-edge was designed to incorporate full-span slats that would automatically open as the aircraft's speed reduced. Speed brakes (powered by hydraulic rams) were designed for each side of the rear fuselage, with an additional brake petal under the fuselage behind the wing trailing edge. However, wind tunnel tests eventually demonstrated that the configuration was unsatisfactory and the design was replaced by a pair of larger brake doors that were fixed into the lower portions of the rear fuselage sides, designed for use at any speed or altitude. The fuselage structure was relatively

The first XP-86 was largely representative of the production-standard F-86A that followed, although the prototype did incorporate some minor differences. Most notably, the aircraft was equipped with large test booms attached to each wing tip. The port wing probe supported pitch and yaw sensors, while the starboard probe was attached to a NACA swiveling pitot head. The standard airspeed detection tube is attached to the fin leading-edge, although it was placed inside the air intake on early F-86A aircraft. Also visible is the engine cooling vent on the side of the port fuselage, which was changed to a twin-vent arrangement (as illustrated) before reverting to single-vent configuration. *(Photos: USAF)*

►▼ **Two views of the first XP-86, illustrating the aircraft's one-piece main undercarriage door and two-piece leading-edge slat arrangement. PU-597 was transferred to the 4901st Support Wing at Kirtland AFB after completing flight test duties with North American Aviation. It was finally moved to Frenchman's Flat on the Nevada Test Site, where it was used as a test airframe for nuclear device testing. It is believed that the aircraft survived at least two nuclear blasts but it was finally removed as part of a site clearance programme In 1965.** ***(Photos: USAF)***

simple, and designed so that the entire rear fuselage could be removed just aft of the wing trailing edge, enabling the engine to be accessed easily. The undercarriage comprised of a simple nose gear leg and wheel, combined with main wheels that retracted inwards into the wing and fuselage structure. The wheel track (width between wheels) was surprisingly narrow, thanks to the need to position external fuel tanks as close to the aircraft centreline as possible. Stability issues prevented the use of wing tip-mounted tanks (as had been proposed for the straight-wing design), and under wing drop tanks had to be fitted as far inboard as possible. The vertical and horizontal tail surfaces were also re-designed to incorporate sweep, the horizontal surfaces retaining their dihedral angle.

The first of the three XP-86 prototypes was 45-59597, and this aircraft was completed on 8 August 1947 at North American's Inglewood headquarters in California. It had taken three years to reach this stage, with some 801,386 engineering hours having been spent on the aircraft, together with 340,594 drafting hours, during which 6,488 engineering orders were issued. Powered by a Chevrolet-manufactured J35-C-3 engine, delivering a modest 4,000lb thrust, the unarmed prototype was unpainted and devoid of any external markings when it emerged into the Californian sunshine to begin initial taxi trials at Mines Field (now the southeastern portion of Los Angeles International Airport). With these tests completed, the aircraft was partially dismantled and transported by road on 10 September to Muroc Army Air Field (now better-known as Edwards AFB) where NAA set up its own Flight Test Section. George Welch was selected to make the P-86's maiden flight. Welch was a hugely experienced pilot, famous as the first pilot to take-off to engage enemy aircraft during the attack on Pearl Harbor in 1941, and having completed his military service, had joined NAA as a test pilot. On 1 October the prototype XP-86 was declared ready for flight and with little fuss or fanfare, the aircraft made its first flight on that day, accompanied by a P-82 chase plane. This would have been uneventful, had it not been for the aircraft's troublesome landing gear. After climbing to 10,000ft, Welch raised the undercarriage but didn't obtain the expected indicator lights on his cockpit instrument panel. Further retraction cycles were performed and the chase plane pilot reported that the landing gear consistently failed to fully retract, and that the nose gear leg would not extend fully at speeds above 130 knots. It was only when Welch reduced power that the gear fully retracted. But after completing the ten-minute flight, the landing gear problems

These photographs provide an interesting comparison between the proportions of the original FJ-1 Fury and the Sabre that was developed directly from it. Although the Sabre retains the Fury's general configuration, the aircraft is in effect a completely different machine, reflected in the comparative performance of the two. *(Photos: US Navy and NASA)*

F-86A 47-631 made its first flight on 15 February 1949. It was then assigned to the 94th FIS at March AFB in California, and remained with that unit until July 1951 when it was withdrawn and assigned to Chanute AFB for use as a ground instructional airframe. *(Photo: USAF)*

returned as the aircraft approached Muroc. The nose when leg failed to fully extend even with the use of the aircraft's emergency system, but Welch decided to land and attempt to hold off the nose wheel for as long as possible after touch-down. The main wheels made contact at 117kt and with the aircraft's nose held high, the nose wheel leg slowly extended as the speed reduced, finally reaching its fully extended position at 78kt. This enabling Welch to lower the nose and complete the landing. Investigations revealed that an incorrect retraction jack was at the root cause of the incident, and repairs were made in preparations for the second flight. This eventually took place on 9 October, although for this and a few subsequent flights, the undercarriage was locked down. North American then embarked upon a short flight test programme of some 30 hours before handing the aircraft to USAF pilots (the AAF became the United States Air Force on 18 September) for further testing. No significant problems were encountered during the initial company test phase and it was the issue of speed that Welch raised as the XP-86's only deficiency. He reported that the J35 engine delivered some 1,000lb less thrust than the J47 engine that was proposed for production aircraft and although this resulted in a relatively disappointing speed performance for the prototype, it indicated that production aircraft would be adequately

F-86A Sabres awaiting delivery to the USAF, at NAA's Inglewood facility (now part of Los Angeles International Airport). F-86A-5-NA 48-204 was assigned to the 71st FS at March AFB before moving to the 115th FIS at Van Nuys Airport. It was written-off in a flying accident during May 1955. *(Photo: NAA)*

powered. In all other respects the XP-86 had performed well, as indicated by Welch's comments after the first flight: "The plane's so clean that you never have trouble. Reduce drag to a minimum and you don't have to worry about effects of compressibility shock waves. Spin recovery is easy when pressure on the elevators is released. On take-off it seems at first as if the nose is pointed too high and you might stall. You soon get used to it though."

The prototype XP-86 temporarily moved to Muroc's north site during December, due to flooding across the main site. It was from the latter base that the first USAF evaluation flights were performed over a period of six days, Major Ken Chilstrom reporting that the aircraft flew very well, although a troublesome cockpit pressurisation system still didn't operate and affected the pilot's oxygen system. After the 77th flight the aircraft was grounded for a thorough engine inspection, and a number of modifications were made at this time, including the substitution of a completely new rear fuselage and tail, incorporating the revised air brake design. Until this stage the prototype had been fitted with the original three-brake layout that had subsequently been abandoned, although the brake doors had been taped shut and were never used. The new brake doors functioned well, although they created severe buffeting at speeds above 400mph. They were however deemed satisfactory at speeds up to 450mph if deployed to only 60% deflection. The prototype was also fitted with an instrumentation boom at this stage, extending some ten feet ahead of the aircraft's nose where speed readings would be unaffected by any shock wave effects. After just eight flights it was established that the aircraft's wing-mounted pitot probes were accurately recording speeds, so the test boom was removed. Some instability problems were experienced which led to a fairly simple modification of the elevator design, incorporating a shorter chord. The aircraft was also subsequently fitted with an Allison-built J35-A-5 engine rated at 3,920lb before eventually being refitted with a production-standard J47. With the Allison-built J35 the prototype was recorded as having a gross weight of 13,790lb, with a top speed of 599mph at sea level and 618mph at 14,0000ft or 575mph at 35,000ft (Mach 0.875). Initial rate of climb was 4,000ft/min and 30,000ft could be reached in 12.1 minutes. Service ceiling was 41.300ft and a typical take-off run required a speed of 125mph and a ground run of 3,020ft. On 19 November 1947 the XP-86 exceeded Mach 1.0 for the first time, thereby becoming the first combat aircraft (at least in the West) to attain supersonic speed, and only the second US aircraft type to exceed the sound barrier. George Welch put the aircraft into a shallow dive from 35,000ft

On 15 September 1948 Major Richard L. Johnson set a new world speed record flying the sixth production F-86A-1-NA Sabre, 47-611, at Muroc AFB. Making four consecutive passes at altitudes between 75-125 ft, the Sabre averaged 670.981 mph. In this rare colour photograph of NAA's Inglewood facility, a batch of F-86A aircraft can also be seen being prepared for delivery to the USAF's 94th FIS at March AFB. ***(Photo: NAA)***

F-86A-1-NA 47-631 shows evidence of some gun-firing, with staining visible around the hinged gun port doors. This aircraft made its first flight on 15 February 1949, flying with the 94th FIS at March AFB until July 1951 when it was withdrawn and delivered to Chanute AFB for use as a ground instructional airframe. ***(Photo: USAF)***

▲◄

Testing of the F-86 continued throughout the early years of the aircraft's development. The eighth F-86 to be built (F-86A-1-NA 47-609) was retained by NAA for flight testing. It was then transferred to NACA (the forerunner of NASA) for further research and development work. It is pictured during 1954 at NACA's Ames Research Facility, undergoing wind tunnel tests to investigate wing design improvements. *(Photos: NASA)*

▲

F-86A-5-NA 48-177 was assigned to the USAF Weapons School at Nellis AFB until March 1952 when it was written-off in a flying accident. The aircraft is fitted with flush fitting gun muzzle doors. These proved to be troublesome and were deleted from late-production F-86A aircraft. *(Photo: Key Collection)*

In 'clean' configuration without any external stores, F-86A-5-NA 48-773 illustrates the forward-folding nosewheel door that was fitted to all production F-86 Sabres. This particular aircraft was assigned to the Silver Sabres Aerobatic Team, formed by the 355th Fighter Squadron in 1949 at Langley AFB. It was written off in a flying accident during the following year. *(Photo: Key Collection)*

Pictured with temporary test booms attached, F-86A-5-NA 48-291 crashed on take-off at Inglewood during October 1949 after having been bailed to NACA as Aircraft No.116. The airframe was returned to USAF ownership for spares recovery. *(Photo: Key Collection)*

Assigned to the 4th FIG and deployed to the Korean theatre, F-86A-5-NA 48-196 was converted to RF-86A standard, with reconnaissance equipment installed in a ventral pannier under the fuselage. This aircraft also served with the 15th TRS (67th TRW) and the 115th FIS, California ANG. *(Photo: Key Collection)*

above Muroc and reportedly achieved Mach 1.02, although North American Aviation was obliged to keep this achievement to itself for some time, thanks to the USAF's (and the US government's) decision to keep supersonic flight secret.

Although Chuck Yeager had gone supersonic for the first time on 14 October, it wasn't until 20 December that news of this event reached the public, courtesy of the *Los Angeles Times*. Some former NAA personnel have suggested that it was in fact the XP-86 that first broke the sound barrier over Muroc, some two weeks before Chuck Yeager, and that politics has buried this achievement for more than 70 years. Al Blackburn (a former NAA test pilot) claims in his book *Aces Wild: The Race for Mach 1* that Yeager almost broke the sound barrier in September 1947 but the aircraft was subsequently grounded for modifications to the aircraft's pitch controls. George Welch reportedly decided to go supersonic on during the XP-86's first flight, albeit on a distinctly unofficial basis without official sanction from either NAA or the USAF. Al Blackburn describes the event in his book as follows: "In a little more than 10 minutes, Welch had reached 35,000 feet. Levelling out, he watched the indicated airspeed climb to 320 knots. He estimated that should be Mach 0.90. He had been heading east and was just passing over the El Mirage dry lake. Rolling into a 40-degree dive, he turned to the west. His aircraft was pointing at Pancho's hacienda [air-racing pilot, Pancho Barnes], several miles south of Rogers Dry Lake. The airspeed indicator seemed to be stuck at about 350 knots, but the Sabre was behaving just fine. At 29,000 feet there was a little wing roll. Correcting the roll, Welch pushed into a steeper dive. The airspeed indicator suddenly jumped to 410 knots and continued to rise. At 25,000 feet he brought the Sabre back to level flight and reduced power. The wing rocked again and the airspeed jumped from

nearly 450 back to 390. Welch pulled up into a barrel roll to the left followed by one to the right, not unlike the victory rolls used in the recent war by returned fighter pilots to let their crews know they had bagged an enemy aircraft. Before he left for Los Angeles to brief the Sabre project people, Welch called Palmer, who reported that a big ba-boom had nearly bounced her out of bed. She added that aviation pioneer Florence Lowe 'Pancho' Barnes, a big Yeager supporter, had heard it too but attributed it to "some mining operation up in the hills."

Palmer (to whom Blackburn refers) was Millie Palmer, a close friend of Welch's. Blackburn's account suggests that Welch had either deliberately exceeded the speed of sound during the XP-86's first flight, or he had inadvertently done so, thanks to the unexpected jumps in the airspeed indicator's readings. What is certain is that Welch had put the aircraft through a series of fairly energetic manoeuvres as part of his attempts to fix the undercarriage retraction problems that had manifested themselves after take-off, therefore it is perhaps possible that the aircraft did indeed reach Mach 1.0 during this time period. But with the undercarriage partially extended for much of the time, it would have been physically impossible to achieve supersonic speed unless a chance combination of hard manoeuvring combined with a brief spell of fully retracted gear to enable the aircraft to momentarily exceed Mach 1.0, causing the reported sonic boom. But if this really is what happened, it is at odds with Blackburn's supposition that Welch had intended to go supersonic during the flight all along. It seems likely that the truth will now never be known, and while the history books attribute the first supersonic flight to Chuck Yeager, some will inevitably continue to speculate that it was in fact the XP-86 that first broke the sound barrier, and not Bell X-1, *Glamorous Glennis*.

The second prototype (45-59598) joined the test programme early in 1948, by which stage the aircraft had been re-designated as the XP-86 (the 'Pursuit' designation having finally been abandoned in June). It was followed by the third XP-86 (45-59599) in May. Both aircraft were essentially similar to the first, with only minor alterations such as the replacement of the BC-453B radio range receiver with AN/ARN-6 radio compass receivers. The first XP-86 was handed over to the USAF on 3 December 1948, followed by the second and third prototypes over the following weeks. While the USAF continued evaluating the XF-86, NAA concentrated its efforts on the production version of the aircraft, the F-86A (initially designated as the P-86A). The production version of the F-86 retained most of the prototype's design features, but the J35 engine was replaced by General Electric's J47-GE-1, nominally rated at 4,850lb thrust. The only obvious external difference when compared to the prototype was the removal of the fin-mounted pitot probe, which was now relocated to the inner surface of the air intake trunk. Less obvious was a re-designed undercarriage bay door for the nose gear, which was now a two-piece folding component. The fin-mounted

During 1954 the 197th Fighter Squadron was re-assigned to the USAF's Air Defense Command. As a component unit of the Arizona Air National Guard, based at Phoenix Airport, the 197th exchanged its F-51 Mustangs for F-86A Sabres, becoming the 197th Fighter Interceptor Squadron. The F-86A remained in use with the unit until 1958 when the all-weather F-86L was introduced into service. ***(Photo: Key Collection)***

ANG
91164
ARIZ
ANG
ANG
91047
ARIZ
ANG
ANG
91070
ARIZ
ANG

The 116th Fighter Squadron was brought to active duty on 1 February 1951. Assigned to the 81st Fighter-Interceptor Group and moved to Moses Lake AFB, Washington, after only four months of training, the 81st FIG was deployed to RAF Shepherds Grove to bolster NATO forces in Europe. It was the first time that a National Guard fighter squadron had crossed to the European Theatre under its own power and only the second time such a move had been attempted without air refuelling. Shortly after arriving in the UK, two Sabres visited de Havilland's factory at Hatfield on a goodwill visit and were photographed by invited media, posing with two of the company's famous aircraft designs. *(Photos: Key Collection)*

navigation lights were relocated on the engine exhaust 'pen nib' fairing, and the wing leading-edge slats were now produced as one-piece items, rather than the two-piece components that had been fitted to the prototypes. As planned, the aircraft incorporated six 0.50 calibre machine guns, each equipped with 300 rounds of ammunition. The guns were positioned in groups of three, either side of the aircraft's cockpit, emerging in the nose section behind the intake lip. In order to preserve the streamlined contours of the aircraft's external surface, the gun muzzles incorporated hinged panels that opened when the guns fired, before closing flush with the fuselage outer surface. Unfortunately, they often failed to function correctly and they were quickly dismissed as being of little value. Despite this, they continued to be incorporated into each F-86A that was manufactured. Some internal changes were also made to the aircraft (including alterations to equipment fitted in the cockpit), but in overall terms the airframe was much the same, albeit with an increased all-up weight of 10,077lb. The aircraft could climb higher and at a faster rate of 7,800ft/min, with a top speed of 585mph at sea level, representing a very significant increase of some 70mph when compared to the first prototype.

North American Aviation employed the USAF's preferred 'block production' system so that changes in modification states could be signified by the aircraft's full designation. Consequently, the first aircraft to be produced were given the company designation NA-151, but officially referred to as the P-86A-1 (later revised to F-86A-1), the '1' denoting the creation of a first 'block' of aircraft produced to the same standard. The second block would be given the designation F-86A-5 and then continue as incremental blocks of five so that any post-production modifications would enable additional block numbers to be employed within these groups of five. Thus, the first aircraft were produced as the P-86A-1-NA with serial numbers 47-605 through to 47-637. The first aircraft to be completed at Inglewood made its first flight from Mines Field (Los Angeles Airport) on 20 May 1948, and on 28 May it was nominally delivered to the USAF in company with the second production machine, although they were swiftly returned to NAA so that they could be employed on initial flight testing duties. The first aircraft to be permanently handed over to the USAF was 47-608, which went to the 3200th Proof Test Group at Eglin AFB on 16 July as an F-86A-1-NA, the 'Pursuit' prefix having been switched to 'Fighter' on 16 July. As more aircraft were completed they were distributed to various sites for testing and evaluation, some going to Muroc, others to Chanute AFB and Wright-Patterson AFB, while some remained with NAA. The USAF was immediately impressed by the F-86 and with the US Navy claiming media headlines with its Douglas Skystreak aircraft (which had achieved a new world air speed record of 650.796mph on 25 August 1947), it wasn't surprising that the USAF was keen to exploit the potential of its new fighter. Plans were made to make a new air speed record attempt during the Cleveland National Air Races in Ohio. F-86A-1-NA 47-608 was selected as a suitable airframe for the record attempt and on 5 September 1948 Major Robert L. Johnson completed six low-level passes (below 165ft) as stipulated by Fédération Aéronautique Internationale (FAI) rules. Despite being witnessed by an audience of more than 80,000, the runs were not properly calibrated and the FAI was unable to certify the record attempt, although readings indicated that an

F-86A-5-NA 49-1193 was delivered to the 334th Fighter Squadron, North Carolina Air National Guard. The unit wasted no time in applying red paint trim to its aircraft. *(Photo: Key Collection)*

F-86A-5-NA 48-1081 wearing the markings of the 165th Fighter Squadron (123rd Fighter Group), Kentucky Air National Guard. This unit operated the F-86A Sabre from 1956 until 1968. *(Photo: Key Collection)*

average speed of 669.480mph had been attained. A second record attempt was made but weather conditions deteriorated, and the USAF abandoned it. Far more benign conditions prevailed at Muroc, and a new record attempt was made there with F-86 A-1-NA 47-611. Major Johnson successfully completed a further six runs (some of which were at a height of just 75ft above the ground) on 14 September, and the FAI recorded the runs at an average speed of 670.981mph, thereby setting a new world air speed record that was some 50mph higher than the figure set by the Navy's distinctly non-production-standard Skystreak.

Although deliveries of F-86As to the USAF began during the summer of 1948, it wasn't until 14 February 1949 that the first operational squadron received its first aircraft, when 47-627 and 47-628 were delivered to March AFB in California, to join the 94th Fighter Squadron (1st Fighter Group). By mid-March the unit had ten aircraft on strength. The aircraft quickly earned an enviable reputation for speed and agility, combined with more than adequate firepower. Pilots were eager to fly the Sabre and although a number of serious accidents occurred during the first year of operations with the 94th FS, only two could be attributed to aircraft deficiencies, and even these were of a mechanical (rather than design) nature. Considering the aircraft's status as a completely new swept-wing jet, this was quite some achievement. By September 1949 the first full batch of 188 full production-standard aircraft (the F-86A-5-NA) had been delivered to the USAF. With a J47-GE-7 engine, this variant incorporated a modified sliding cockpit canopy that could be jettisoned in an emergency. The windshield design was changed, and external weapons pylons were fitted under each wing, capable of carrying either a 1,000lb bomb or a 206gal fuel tank.

Other less obvious modifications included heating for the gun bays, fire-resistant oil tanks and lines, and an improved nose wheel steering system. Modifications were also made to the wing slat design, as operational experience (and particularly spin testing) had revealed how the aerodynamic forces on the wing leading edges caused the slats to slam in and out with great force. Various 'fixes' were employed until a satisfactory arrangement was installed in F-86A 48-211 and all subsequent aircraft, enabling the wing slats to move in and out automatically and smoothly. It was the 1st Fighter Group that bestowed the name 'Sabre' upon the F-86. Until February 1949 the aircraft had sometimes been referred-to as the 'Silver Charger' by personnel at Inglewood (as a suitable follow-on to the P-51 Mustang), but when the 1st FG organised a naming contest, some 78 entries were received and 'Sabre' was selected as the winner, and this was approved by the USAF on 4 March, although for some time the national media mistakenly continued to refer to the aircraft as the 'Sabrejet', having misunderstood how the aircraft was inevitably referred to as a 'jet' by USAF officials.

In March 1949 some 17 F-86As were delivered to the 31st Fighter Escort Wing at Turner AFB in Georgia, although these were soon transferred to the 1st Fighter Group at March AFB following a change in USAF planning. On 7 June 1949 the first two aircraft for the 4th Fighter Group at Langley AFB in Virginia were delivered, followed by a further seven aircraft a couple of days later. In August, the 81st Fighter Group at Kirtland AFB in New Mexico began to re-equip with Sabres and together these three Fighter Groups assumed responsibility for the air defence of large regions of the continental USA. Meanwhile, NAA had received an order for 333 more aircraft on 23 February, under contract AC-21671 for aircraft powered by a J47-GE-13 engine, rated at 5,200lb thrust. These aircraft (F-86A-5) were designated as the NA-161 by NAA and later aircraft in this batch were equipped with slightly modified ailerons incorporating a shorter chord, together with improved elevator boost. Early in 1950 the 33rd FIW at Otis AFB began to re-equip with the Sabre, followed by the 56th Fighter Group at Selfridge AFB. Later that year the 23rd FIW at Presque Isle AFB also received Sabres, completing the re-equipment of the USAF's multi-squadron fighter wings. Throughout this period a variety of upgrade programmes were put into action, enabling early-production Sabres to be brought up to the latest standards. Most importantly, the majority of early Sabres were re-fitted with the more powerful J47-GE-13 engine, many being modified in situ at their unit bases, although many other Sabres were returned to NAA for modification and overhaul at the company's Long Beach facility. It was at this site that most of the early-production Sabres were fitted with new forward fuselage panels incorporating simplified gun muzzle fairings that dispensed with the troublesome doors. Likewise, the pitot probe that had been relocated to the inside of the air intake, was shifted to the port wing tip, after experience had shown how pressure variations inside the air intake could affect the accuracy of the pitot reading.

With the initial equipment of operational units completed, attention turned to training, and on 13 March 1950 the 3595th Pilot Training Wing at Las Vegas AFB began to acquire the Sabre. In October (by which stage the station had become Nellis AFB) the unit was fully equipped, and initial plans were made to begin the re-equipment of the 2525th PTW at Williams AFB, although the few aircraft assigned to this unit were transferred to Nellis after only a few weeks. The 3595th PTW had a troubled relationship with the Sabre. Tasked with the conversion of relatively inexperienced pilots onto a very potent machine, it was hardly surprising that a large number of flying accidents occurred, although it is fair to say that most of the early Sabre losses with this and other USAF units were often due to causes that could not be directly attributed to the aircraft itself. In general terms, the Sabre was in fact a very reliable machine that performed remarkably well – possibly a little too well for the unwary. Other USAF units to acquire the Sabre soon followed. The 15th FIS at Davis Monthan AFB and the 469th FIS at McGhee-Tyson AFB both re-equipped with the F-86A. The 81st Fighter Interceptor Wing (based at Larson AFB in Washington) was first prepared for overseas deployment early in 1951, and in addition to its component 91st FIS and 92nd FIS, the Wing also embraced the 116th FIS (Air National Guard) for a mass transfer across the Atlantic to Britain with a large fleet of F-86As. The first aircraft departed in August via Goose Bay, Iceland and Stornoway and by 5 September the 8st FIW was fully deployed to RAF Bentwaters in Suffolk. The 91st FIS remained at that site while the 92nd FIS and 116th FIS deployed to RAF Shepherds Grove, the 116th FIS returning to the US in November 1952, to be replaced by the 78th FIS. This deployment marked the arrival of the Sabre in Europe and also the beginning of a very long stay in the United Kingdom by the 81st FIW that finally ended (as the 81st FW) in 1993. However the Sabres didn't stay for quite so long, and after being replaced by Thunderstreaks during 1954 they were returned to the United States as ship cargo. ❖

FIGHTING FORCE

The Korean War begins and the F-86 Sabre goes into battle

F-86-5-NA 48-160 wearing the markings of the 115th Fighter Bomber Squadron, California Air National Guard. *(Photo: USAF)*

This rare colour image of an early F-86A was captured by North American Aviation's staff photographer during 1950. 47-630 was assigned to the 27th FIS (1st FIG) until September 1955 when the aircraft was struck off charge. It was then transferred to Chanute AFB for use as a ground instructional airframe. *(Photo: NAA)*

It was on 25 June 1950 that North Korea's Army crossed the 38th Parallel and invaded South Korea. Communism was sweeping across the region and the United States was poised to intervene. But despite having forged ahead with the development of jet engines and high-performance combat aircraft, the USAF was at its lowest strength since the darkest days of 1941. Just over 400 Sabres were in service together with 600 F-84 Thunderjets and 800 F-80 Shooting Stars, but from a total strength of almost 5,500 fighter aircraft, some two-thirds were of obsolescent wartime origin. Despite having in excess of 3,000 bombers, only 400 of these were of post-war vintage. The reason for this deplorable situation was easy to identify – the USAF was prepared to defend the continental USA (and therefore, Europe too) from attack but it was totally unprepared to counter any other type of threat. The Korean War literally came out of the blue, and such was the USAF's unpreparedness for a conflict in this region that the first five months of the ensuing Korean War saw the USAF deploy mostly surplus World War Two aircraft such as the F-51 Mustang, B-26 Invader and B-29. Of course the USAF did have forces stationed in the region, in the shape of the Far East Air Force (FEAF) based in Japan and the Philippines. Equipped with F-80C Shooting Stars, F-82 Twin Mustangs and B-26 Invaders, the force was backed up by B-29 bombers based in Guam. The North Korean Air Force was, by comparison, in a deplorable state. With only surplus aircraft that had been supplied by Russia, its combat force comprised only 70 Yak-9 and La-11 fighters, together with 62 Il-10 bombers. However the South Korean Air Force was virtually non-existent, with only 16 trainer aircraft at its disposal. Clearly, North Korean High Command did not anticipate taking on the United States, but it is fair to say that the USAF never expected to be fighting in Korea either. On 28 June the US agreed to assist the South Korean government and USAF operations duly began, attacking the columns of advancing North Korean forces. The American FEAF quickly defeated the NKAF and air supremacy was swiftly achieved for both the US and the United Nations forces that had been assembled, in co-operation with Britain, Australia, South Africa, Turkey and other countries. The situation on the ground was far more problematical, but by the end of September the Korean War was effectively over, with communist forces having successfully been pushed back to the north. However, the UN's decision to "ensure conditions of stability throughout Korea" required American forces to continue driving northwards, in spite of warnings from China that if the US crossed the 38th Parallel, it would be forced to enter into the conflict. By the end of October, American forces reached the Yalu River at the Chinese and Korean frontier.

On 1 November a formation of F-51 Mustangs (together with a T-6 forward air controller aircraft) was operating over the region when it was suddenly attacked by six unidentified jet fighters. A brief skirmish ensued in which the F-51 pilots employed some hard evasive manoeuvring before escaping from the situation and dashing home. The USAF pilots reported that the shiny silver aircraft had swept wings and were unlike anything that they had encountered before. Over the following days a number of similar events followed, in which the same jet fighters appeared from beyond the Chinese border, diving down to attack any aircraft that happened to be in the region, before heading back over the border where they could not be chased (rules forbade UN and US aircraft from crossing the frontier). It soon became obvious that these mysterious aircraft were in fact Russian-built MiG-15 jets, operated by the Chinese Communist Air Force, and further reports of encounters with them revealed that they were indeed wearing the national insignia of that country. It was evident from the outset that the USAF's F-51 Mustangs were no match for these sleek jet fighters, and the only option that was open to the USAF pilots was to escape from any encounters as swiftly as possible. Far more worrying was how the

A busy scene at North American's Inglewood factory, as F-86Es near completion, prior to delivery to the United States Air Force. *(Photo: Key Collection)*

MiG-15 soon demonstrated that it was also more than a match for even the F-80 Shooting Star, when on 8 November 1950 a flight of four F-80s on a bomber escort mission came face-to-face with four MiG-15s, resulting in what became the first example of all-jet aerial combat. The American pilots spotted the MiG-15s heading for the Chinese border but as the formation broke, USAF pilot Lt. Russell J. Brown managed to intercept the trailing MiG-15, forcing the Chinese pilot to enter into a climbing turn, as Brown struggled to fire at it. The MiG-15 then went into a dive and Brown successfully delivered a lethal burst of machine gun fire, destroying the aircraft moments before it reached the border. This first all-jet encounter had been a victory for the USAF but Brown accepted that he had been lucky. It was abundantly clear to the F-80 pilots that the MiG-15 was considerably faster than the American jets, and possessed a much better rate of climb.

On 26 November the Chinese launched an offensive, driving UN forces south. The MiG-15s continued to appear, and when they began to attack (and sometimes destroy) USAF B-29 bombers, the situation began to look increasingly alarming. The USAF would have to send more aircraft into the region as quickly as possible, and so the 27th Fighter Escort Wing (with F-84E Thunderjets) was ordered to deploy. At the same time, the 4th Fighter Interceptor Wing, complete with its fleet of F-86A Sabres, was similarly ordered into action as part of Operation Straw Boss, and on 11 November the first of the unit's aircraft flew to NAS North Island, from where they were loaded on board the escort carrier *Cape Esperance*, with further aircraft being carried by a tanker vessel. By 13 December the 4th FIS was successfully established at Kisarazu in Japan and after a short 'shake-down' period the first aircraft were deployed into the Korean theatre at Kimpo. The inaugural Sabre combat mission took place on 17 December (coincidentally, the anniversary of the Wright Brothers' first flight at Kitty Hawk) and although it proved to be uneventful, a second sortie flown later the same day resulted in the first encounter with the MiG-15. Patrolling at 32,000ft along the Yalu River, Lt Col Bruce Hinton (commander of the 336th FS) opted to slow his formation of Sabres to 400 knots, in order to give the impression to enemy radar observers that his formation comprised of elderly F-51 Mustangs. This was possibly successful as four MiG-15s duly appeared some 7,000ft below, although they continued on track under the Sabres, presumably because the MiG-15 pilots were either unaware of the Sabres above them, or because they assumed that a formation of Mustangs was not a serious threat. The Sabre pilots jettisoned their external fuel tanks and dived towards the MiGs, and as the MiGs split to evade the attack, Hinton turned in behind the lead aircraft's wingman and opened fire. Firing a burst of 1,500 rounds of machine gun ammunition, smoke began to appear from the MiG's jet pipe, after which flames erupted and the MiG rolled over onto its back before entering into a spin. It crashed and exploded just a few seconds later some ten miles south of the Yalu River.

Further engagements between the F-86 and the MiG-15 were equally successful for the USAF, although the Sabre pilots were aware that their victories were by no means due to any perceived superiority of the F-86. In fact, the Sabre was in some ways inferior to the MiG-15 and it was the skill of the USAF pilots (many of whom were World War Two veterans) that gave the Sabres an important edge over the Chinese Air Force fighters. Although the Chinese pilots were mostly inexperienced, the MiG-15 was a remarkable machine. It possessed a climb rate of some 10,100ft/min as compared to the Sabre's 7,470ft/min, and boasted a service ceiling of 51,500ft, in contrast to the Sabre's more modest 48,000ft. Likewise, the Sabre could attain a top speed of 679mph at sea level, which was a useful 11mph faster than the MiG-15. However at 35,000ft, the Sabre's top speed of 601mph was some 24mph slower than the MiG-15. By any standards the MiG-15 outperformed the Sabre, but with a combination of experience and skill, the USAF managed to maintain superiority, and by the middle of 1951 some 3,550 missions had been flown during which 22 victories had been claimed, with no Sabre losses. Even so, some Sabres had been destroyed, but not as a direct result of aerial combat. Perhaps the most unusual example of this took place on 17 June when a single Po-2 biplane drifted over the parked line of Sabres belonging to the 355th FS, delivering a small bomb that severely damaged eight aircraft, plus a second bomb that completely destroyed one F-86A. Another remarkable fact was that the USAF Sabre pilots had for some time been flying combat missions against Soviet pilots, even though they didn't know it. At the same time as the F-86 first arrived in Korea, a decision had been made to send the Soviet 64th Fighter Aviation Corps to the region, in order to support communist China and to 'field-test' the MiG-15 in combat conditions. The Soviet pilots flew MiG-15s painted with Chinese insignia, wore Chinese uniforms, and (at least for a time) even used only the Korean language for radio communications.

By 1952 the Chinese forces had started to change tactics, and the Korean theatre began to be used as a training area in which relatively inexperienced Chinese pilots could hone their combat skills. Units were

Two factory photographs, illustrating F-86E-10-NA 51-2778 shortly after completion at NAA's Inglewood factory. This parking area (complete with jet blast walls) eventually became part of the ever-expanding Los Angeles International Airport, and this historic site has now become lost amongst the south-eastern portions of the airport. 51-2778 joined the 16th FIS (51st FIG) and deployed to Korea, where it crashed in October 1952 following an engine fire. ***(Photos: NAA)***

FU-158
U.S AIR FORCE
91158
USAF
FU-276
91276
FU-251
91251
FU-261
FU-236

F-86A Sabres assigned to the 336th Fighter Interceptor Squadron (better-known as the 'Rocketeers') pictured at Suwon in 1951 during the Korean War. The black and white wing and fuselage markings were applied in order for pilots to easily distinguish between MiG-15s and Sabres during aerial combat. As can be seen, conditions in Korea were primitive and many airfield sites relied upon PSP (pierced steel planking) runways and parking areas, while personnel were accommodated in tents. *(Photo: USAF)*

progressively trained to a proficient standard and then replaced by new ones to repeat the training process. But even though the Chinese pilots were often raw novices, they were no less aggressive than their more experienced counterparts. The air war continued at a fierce pace, and on the ground the opposing forces continued to battle, even though the frontline positions changed very little. The communist forces often mounted raids against the South Koreans, and these sudden incursions inevitably required air power to break up the conflict. Although the Sabre was ostensibly a fighter, it was also called upon to perform countless ground attack missions – for example, some 3,044 tons of bombs were dropped during the month of June in 1953. The war dragged on, hampered by prisoner repatriation issues, and it wasn't until 27 July 1953 that fighting officially ended. With hindsight it is clear that the outcome was a close-run victory (if it could be called a victory at all) for America and her allies. The ground war could never have been won without air superiority, and with the immensely capable MiG-15 at their disposal, the communist forces could confidently take-on any other aeroplane, apart from the Sabre. But it would be wrong to conclude that the Sabre gave the USAF any clear advantage over the communists. It was the USAF's experience, training and tactical fighting ability that eventually delivered aerial supremacy, and the Sabre simply enabled the USAF to take on the Chinese and Russian pilots on a near-equal basis. But it is also the case that without the Sabre, the Korean War would undoubtedly have been decisively lost.

To understand precisely how the Sabre enabled the USAF to achieve aerial superiority in Korea, it is useful to read the personal accounts from the pilots who flew the deadly missions in the Korean theatre. Col. Francis Gabreski scored six victories

Pictured over Edwards AFB during early flight testing, F-86E-10-NA 51-2849 was eventually assigned to the 25th FIS (51st FIG) and was deployed to Korea in 1952. It was abandoned in the Yellow Sea on 21 November of that year after being ditched by its pilot, the aircraft having sustained battle damage. *(Photo: USAF)*

Colour photographs of the F-86A are comparatively rare. F-86A-5-NA 49-1262 was operated by the 94th Fighter Squadron, based at March AFB in California. As one of the earliest Sabres to enter USAF service, it is believed that this aircraft was not assigned to the Korean theatre. *(Photo: USAF)*

against the MiG-15 during the Korean War and became one of only six American pilots to attain 'Ace' status in the conflict:

"On my fifth mission I got my first MiG. We were on a top cover assignment for the F-84s, which were to strafe airfields in the area of Pyongyang. We took off on a direct vector, climbing into the north. It was only 140 miles and before we were half way, our radar network informed us that bandits were heading down from the Yalu. We spread out more and kept climbing, and we were now over 30,000 feet. It was a perfectly clear day with no clouds but we didn't see the fighter bombers. It was only 25 minutes to the target and as we moved into the area my wingman spotted contrails in the sky ahead and called me over the radio. There were seven or eight contrails at 11 o'clock, much higher than we were. I transmitted 'Eagle Leader here. Bandits eleven o'clock high. Advanced throttles. We'll climb to contrail level and level off just underneath'. The contrails were far away up north. I didn't think these were the aircraft our radar had warned us about, but I warned the others to keep them in sight while we made a 360-degree climbing circle over Pyongyang. We reached 35,000 feet and leveled off and continued to circle. At that moment, we saw directly beneath us, at about 10,000 feet, twelve MiGs flying north. I immediately increased our right bank to come down on them from behind, and by the time we completed the turn they were almost out of sight – that's the thing about jets. We were closing when I spotted them, at about a thousand miles an hour! I told the guys to keep their eyes on the other contrails up north, and we flew back and forth over Pyongyang. We did this until it was almost time to go home. Then we saw a lone MiG heading north below us at 10,000 feet. We were flying west and I positioned the flight by a quick ninety-degree turn to come down from behind him. We went after him as fast as we could but by the time that we were on his course, coming from behind, he was a good six miles ahead of us. I had the throttle wide

The Sabre claimed a number of performance records during the 1950s. On 17 August 1951 Colonel Fred Ascani (vice commander of the Air Force Flight Test Center at Edwards AFB) used F-86E Sabres 51-2721 and 51-2724 (both taken from the NAA production line) to set a new world air speed record. Flying 51-2721, he averaged a speed of 635.69mph and set a new record, receiving the Thompson and MacKay Trophies in recognition of his achievement.

The 4th Fighter Interceptor Wing was the first USAF unit to commit F-86 Sabres to the Korean War and the unit's pilots eventually downed 502 enemy aircraft during the conflict. As can be seen in this picture of aircraft from the 335th FIS taken in April 1952, the early F-86A and later F-86E were both used by the Wing. *(Photo: USAF)*

Numerous Sabres received personalised artwork and names during the Korean War, some aircraft sporting two names simultaneously. F-86A FU-217 *Honey Bucket* or *Every Man a Tiger* was eventually converted to RF-86A standard for reconnaissance duties, based in Japan. Assigned to 15th Tactical Reconnaissance Squadron, 67th Tactical Reconnaissance Wing, the aircraft was shot down by ground fire on 27 June 1952. *(Photo: USAF)*

open with a maximum Mach of 0.91. I wanted to overtake him before arriving at minimum fuel for return, but the stern chase seemed like an hour. It was probably only minutes. Finally I was in position some 1,000 feet behind. He was on a steady course and his MiG was painted red at the nose and had a red rudder. Otherwise it was a dirty aluminum grey. I had two Sabres on the left and one on the right, and we had closed our formation a bit. It was time to pull up the nose and line him up in my sight from below. When the sight was squarely on his mid section, I fired a short burst of armour piercing and incendiary, from the six-fifties. I could see strikes all over the lower section of the fuselage. I kept firing for a couple of seconds and I was now directly astern, about 600 feet back. I centred the sight on his tail pipe and gave him another burst. I saw strikes again, around the engine as well as the wings. Now he went into a slight dive and smoke began to streak back from the tail pipe. I passed over him and broke off to the right and he started down while I kept him in view. He was losing altitude but to my amazement, was still under control. I decided to make another pass from above right. My three Sabres were now strung out behind me. There was grey smoke from the MiG – he had decelerated. In a matter of seconds I closed for another pass, coming in from astern. I got very close and gave him a good, long burst. This time pieces of his aircraft began to fly off. The canopy flew off. Then the pilot ejected. His parachute opened.

F-86E-10-NA 51-27222 joined the 4th Fighter Wing during October 1951. Flown in Korea by Major William Thomas, he named the aircraft *Virginia Belle* and downed a MiG-15 whilst flying it in May 1952. The same aircraft was also used to destroy two more MiG-15s during September of that year. *(Photo: USAF)*

We turned on course for home. I was surprised to see how hard it was to bring down a jet, and how much damage he absorbed before he finally went down. Later of course, we got the bigger guns in the Sabres. These were fifty calibre shells. It took a lot of them to bring one down".

As the Korean War progressed, the F-86 gradually developed into a more capable fighting machine. Back in 1948 the initial testing of the XP-86 had revealed some worrying instability at high speeds, caused by the aircraft's elevator and tailplane design. Various 'fixes' were tried to solve this problem but no truly satisfactory solution was found, the F-86A being manufactured with modified (extended trailing edge) elevators that were only a partial solution to the instability problem. But by the time that the F-86A rolled off the production line, it had been established that an 'all-flying tail' would resolve the instability issue. Instead of

Fourteen F-86Es from the 25th Fighter Interceptor Squadron taxi to the runway for a mission from their base at Suwon in Korea. The PSP (pierced steel planking) taxi track is clearly visible. *(Photo: USAF)*

employing a conventional tailplane with a hinged elevator surface, the entire horizontal surface would be designed to rotate, thereby increasing control effectiveness considerably. The idea had been studied by NACA (the forerunner of NASA) at Langley and had been employed on the Bell XS-1, arguably on the basis of information that had been gleaned from British designers working on the stillborn Miles M.52. North American decided to introduce the new design on all subsequent Sabres, resulting in the F-86E. The F-86B designation was applied to a batch of F-86As that were to have featured a wider fuselage to accommodate more efficient wheels and tyres, but when this requirement was dropped, these became F-86A block 5 aircraft. The F-86C-L variants were very different aircraft, as described later. Design work on the F-86E (the NA-170) began in November 1949, resulting in a contract (AF-9456) for 60 F-86E-1 and 51 F-86E-5 aircraft, issued on 17 January 1950. The new Sabre variant was largely similar to the F-86A, although the rear fuselage shape was changed slightly to feature a flattened strake, leading to a point where the new all-moving tailplane was attached. This was a minor modification, designed to improve the aerodynamic flow around the tail area and not (as was often suggested) to house a tailplane actuator. This was located centrally under the fin, linked to a crossbeam. Internally however, there was a significant change, with the F-86A's manual flying controls having been replaced by a hydraulic system (with spring-loaded artificial feel), and only the rudder remaining under direct mechanical connection. The J47-GE-13 engine was selected for the F-86E, rated at 5,450lb thrust, and (in line with late-production F-86As) a new A-1CM gun sight was installed, together with AN/APG-30 radar. With these modifications the F-86E was 400lb heavier than its predecessor, although service ceiling, range and initial climb rate were all slightly improved. Because the changes to the F-86E were relatively small, no prototype was produced and the first aircraft (50-579) completed its maiden flight on 23 September 1950. Deliveries to the USAF began in February 1951, just weeks after the last F-86As. Some of the initial production aircraft were temporarily retained by NAA for testing and evaluation, but in April 1951 the first examples were delivered to Air Defense Command, when the 97th FIS (Wright-Patterson AFB) and 23rd FIW (Presque Isle AFB) received their first aircraft. The 60th FIS at Otis AFB acquired its first F-86Es in November, but by this stage aircraft were

Although the Sabre is inevitably acclaimed as a fighter, the aircraft was also employed in the ground support role during the Korean War, with some considerable success. This USAF photo illustrates the F-86E's ability to carry not only external fuel tanks, but also high explosive free-fall bombs, in addition to its standard gun armament housed in the forward fuselage. ***(Photo: USAF)***

F-86E-10-NA joined the 25th FIS (51st FIG) during 1951 and was swiftly transported to Korea. It operated in theatre until only May of the following year, when it was shot down during combat with MiG-15s off the Korean coast. ***(Photo: USAF)***

already being sent directly to Korea, where the 4th FIW began transitioning from the F-86A in August 1951. By October the USAF had decided to re-equip a second wing in Korea (the 51st FIW) but NAA was unable to meet the production capacity that this required. As a result, the 23rd FIW and 97th FIS donated many of their aircraft, and the 97th FIS was obliged to temporarily revert to F-86A operations until further F-86Es could be delivered. The capacity issue eventually resulted in a final batch of F-86Es being produced not by NAA but by Canadian manufacturer Canadair. This company had already commenced licence production of the Sabre for Canadian service, but with Inglewood already working at capacity, a requirement for more F-86Es in Korea (needed largely in response to the faster MiG-15bis variant that appeared shortly after the first F-86Es arrived in Korea) meant that further production had to be outsourced. The resulting batch of 60 F-86E-CAN aircraft was delivered to NAA's Fresno facility, where additional USAF equipment was fitted before the airframes were shipped to Korea. Ultimately, a huge number of F-86Es found their way into the Korean theatre, and by the end of 1951 the 51st FIW had re-equipped with Sabres, having transferred its less-than-adequate F-80 Shooting Stars to the 8th FBW.

The F-86F became the ultimate expression of the Sabre design as a day fighter. Created as a more powerful version of the existing F-86E, it was equipped with the J47-EG-27 engine, delivering 5,970lb thrust, and NAA began to develop this variant in July 1950 as the NA-172. A contract was placed (AF-14801) on 11 April 1951 for 109 F-86F airframes, increasing to 360 machines as of 30 June. However, development of the engine didn't go as smoothly as planned and even as thrust output gradually increased, the engine's weight also rose by some 80lb. Delays eventually resulted in the first 132 aircraft being delivered as F-86s, with a J47-GE-13 engine, and it wasn't until 19 March 1952 that the first F-86F-1 (51-2850) made its first flight. Externally similar to the F-86E, the F-86F differed only by the inclusion of a flat windscreen, although this had also been incorporated into the last batch of F-86Es. Internally, the aircraft featured a gun sight-mounted camera and modifications to carry AN-M10 chemical tanks on the external wing pylons. The first completed examples of the F-86F were initially scheduled to go to the 94th FIS, but with the Korean War still a

Pictured during pre-delivery flight trials in 1952, F-86F-5-NA 51-2932 was eventually transferred to the Taiwanese Air Force. ***(Photo: USAF)***

F-86F-30-NA Sabres at Kimpo Air Base in Korea with thr 36th FBW during 1952. The yellow fuselage band outlined in black (also applied to the wing tips) became a standard identification marking for all Sabres in the Korean theatre. *(Photo: USAF)*

priority, they were swiftly re-allocated to the 126th FIS, Wisconsin ANG, in preparation for overseas deployment. The first aircraft was delivered in April 1952 and most of the subsequent airframes to be completed were transferred directly to Japan by sea, and assigned to the 51st FIW during June, followed by the 4th FIW in September. Meanwhile attention had turned towards the creation of additional production capacity. NAA had obtained permission to acquire the former Curtiss factory at Columbus in Ohio during 1950, and after a great deal of preparation, production of F-86Fs began there in December 1950 in anticipation of contract AF-18988 (issued 6 September 1951) for 441 machines, designated as the NA-176 by NAA. While work got underway there, over at Inglewood NAA moved to the F-86F-5, featuring modifications that enabled the aircraft to carry a larger 200gal external drop tank under each wing, instead of the then-standard 120gal version, extending the Sabre's range from 330 miles to 463 miles. Further refinements were developed, including the F-86F-10, with a new A-4 gun sight and a re-located gun camera. Thanks to further delays in the production of the J47-GE-27 engines, the final 100 aircraft in the NA-172 contract could not be completed to F-86F standard, and 97 machines were duly finished as F-86E-15 airframes powered by J47-GE-13 engines, until production of F-86Fs again resumed for the last seven aircraft. During May 1952 the first F-86Fs began to emerge from the Columbus factory, designated as the F-86F-20-NH, and featuring a small number of only minor modifications. Despite this, production at the new facility was slow, and the last aircraft for the contract wasn't completed until January 1953.

F-86F-30-NA Sabre 52-4446 *Terrible Turtle* with the 35th Fighter Bomber Squadron 'Black Panthers', 8th FBW. *(Photo: USAF)*

During the previous year, another significant stage in the Sabre's history unfolded. NAA maintained an interest in developing the aircraft's handling and performance still further, and various wing design modifications were studied. These investigations eventually resulted in a new wing that was flight-tested on three Sabres during August 1952. The familiar leading-edge slat assembly was removed and replaced by a fixed leading edge that incorporated a forward extension of 6in at the wing root and 3in at the wing tip, increasing the wing area from 287.9 square feet to 302.3 square feet. Colloquially, the new design soon became known as the '6-3'

◄ A busy scene at an unidentified USAF base with a lone F-86F-20-NA Sabre parked amongst a huge number of F-86D all-weather interceptors. *(Photo: USAF)*

◄ 36th Fighter Bomber Squadron F-86F-30-NA 52-4406 was named *Miss Chuckles*, with titles applied under the cockpit on the side of the fuselage. *(Photo: USAF)*

▼ F-86F-35-NA Sabre 52-5233, proudly wearing the markings of the 72nd Fighter Bomber Squadron. In 1958 this aircraft was transferred to the Royal Norwegian Air Force and remained in Norway until 1967 when it was returned to the USAF and placed in storage at Davis-Monthan AFB. It was scrapped during 1968. *(Photo: USAF)*

wing. In addition to the removal of the slats, the new wing also featured a 5in-high fence that was fixed at the 70 per cent span position, designed to reduce span-wise airflow over the wing surfaces. The new wing improved the Sabre's performance quite considerably, raising top speed from 688mph to 695mph at sea level, and from 604mph to 608mph at 35,000ft – a more modest improvement but a useful one when the Sabre was being pitted against the speedy MiG-15. Perhaps more importantly, the new wing enabled the aircraft to perform tighter turns at altitude, although on the debit side, it increased stalling speed from 128mph to 144mph, combined with a more sudden and violent stall at that speed. From September 1952 the new wing was made available in kit form, to be shipped out to Korea where aircraft could be converted in theatre and eventually of of the F-86Fs in Korea were modified to '6-3' standard, while the wing was incorporated into F-86F production, starting with the 171st F-86F-25 (51-13341) and the 200th F-86F-30 (52-4505). USAF Sabre pilots soon discovered that the new wing enabled the F-86F to out-perform the MiG-15 in both speed and turning ability, although the MiG still retained an altitude advantage. Unfortunately, many Sabre pilots failed to appreciate the low-speed stall attributes of the new wing and many accidents ensued until pilots became familiarised with the Sabre's slightly different handling properties – both good and bad.

Although designed purely as a fighter and interceptor, the Korean War soon put additional demands upon the Sabre, and the USAF was soon keen to develop the aircraft into a more versatile fighter-bomber. Work on the NA-191 began in October 1951, in an effort to equip the Sabre with additional external stores capability. Until now, the aircraft had been capable of carrying an external fuel tank under each wing or a bomb

During March 1954 the 15th TRS deployed to Komaki Air Base in Japan, receiving eight newly-modified 'Haymaker' RF-86 Sabres. With these aircraft, it secretly overflew Soviet, North Korean and communist Chinese territory during the mid-1950s. RF-86F 52-4492 participated in these critical overflight missions. It was transferred to the Republic of Korea Air Force (ROKAF) in 1958, and remained there into the 1980s. Arriving at the USAF Museum in 1998 for restoration, it was placed on display in 2005, repainted in 15th TRS markings. *(Photo: USAF)*

of up to 1,000lb. But it was clearly evident that it needed to be capable of carrying both if it was to achieve its full potential. NAA designers eventually devised provision for a second weapons pylon that was positioned inboard of the existing pylon position, and capable of carrying either a 120gal drop tank or a 1,000lb bomb. This gave the Sabre a ferry range of some 1,600 miles if all four pylons were to carry fuel tanks, but more importantly, it enabled the type to carry bombs while retaining adequate combat range capability. As a fighter-bomber, the NA-191 received a modified flight control system with improved longitudinal stability and reduced stick forces for the pilot. Contract AF-6517 was issued on 5 August 1952 for 907 aircraft to be manufactured at Inglewood, together with 341 NA-176 aircraft from the Columbus factory (another 259 aircraft were added to the Columbus contract a few weeks later). Although outwardly different to previous variants, they were designated as the F-86F-30-NA and F-86F-35NA (Inglewood) and F-86F-25-NH (Columbus). When the first aircraft began to appear in October 1952 they were immediately sent to Korea, but when the Columbus-built machines emerged, the majority went to units in the USA and many were prepared for deployment to Europe. Delays resulted in the first fighter-bomber Sabres arriving in Korea during January 1953, the first aircraft joining the 18th FBW at Osan. The 12th FBS re-equipped in March, followed by South Africa's No 2 Squadron. By the end of July FEAF had 132 F-86F fighter-bombers in theatre and these, together with the F-86E and F-86F fighters – remained active in theatre until the very last days of the Korean War.

Mention should also be made of another Sabre variant that made a significant contribution to the Korean War, despite often being overlooked. The USAF's RF-80A and

▲
F-86F-30-NA Sabre 52-4808 was initially allocated to the 4th Fighter Group and deployed to the Korean theatre, where it was subsequently converted to RF-86F reconnaissance standard, joining the 15th TRS (67th TRW). It was withdrawn at Kisarazu Air Base in Japan and dismantled. *(Photo: USAF)*

◄
F-86F-6-CAN 51-2881 was a former RCAF Sabre Mk.2, transferred to the USAF in 1952. It joined the 39th FIS (51st FIW) and after service in Korea it was transferred to the 104th FIS (Maryland ANG) and finally the 191st FIS (Utah ANG) before being placed in storage at Davis Monthan AFB in 1959. *(Photo: USAF)*

▼
F-86F-30-NA Sabre 52-4584 was flown by US Marine Corps Major John H. Glenn and dubbed *MiG Mad Marine* during service in Korea. Glenn flew this aircraft during his time as an exchange pilot with the 25th Fighter Squadron, 51st Fighter Wing, during 1953. He shot down three MiG-15s during his time in theatre. He later became an astronaut and a US senator. *(Photo: USAF)*

▲
F-86F-30-NA Sabre 52-4363 from the 12th Fighter Bomber Squadron, 18th Fighter Bomber Wing, at Taegu Air Base in Korea, during 1952. *(Photo: USAF)*

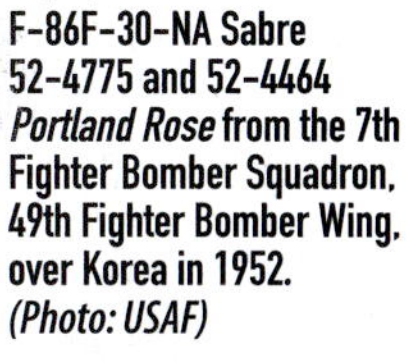

◄▼
F-86F-30-NA Sabre 52-4775 and 52-4464 *Portland Rose* from the 7th Fighter Bomber Squadron, 49th Fighter Bomber Wing, over Korea in 1952. *(Photo: USAF)*

F-86F-30-NA 52-4432 serving with the 12th Fighter Bomber Squadron (18th FBW) at Formosa, with the unit's markings applied across the aircraft's tail fin. In the background is a Chinese Nationalist Air Force F-84G Thunderjet. ***(Photo: USAF)***

RB-45C Tornado reconnaissance aircraft could not operate unescorted in a region where MiGs were active, and a faster platform was needed. No reconnaissance version of the F-86 was being planned by either NAA or the USAF, but several pilots from the 67th Tactical Reconnaissance Wing at Kimpo AB obtained permission to convert some F-86s to the reconnaissance role, under Project Honeybucket. Two F-86As (48-187 and 48-217) were ferried to Tachikawa in Japan for conversion. There was little room inside an F-86 fuselage for the long-range cameras necessary for the reconnaissance mission. However, it was found that if the lower pair of 0.50in guns on the port side of the fuselage was removed, there was enough space for a small focal length K-25 camera taken from the RB-26C. The camera was mounted horizontally, but a series of mirrors allowed it to shoot vertically out of a small opening cut into the port side of the Sabre's nose. The first modified F-86As were returned to Kimpo in October 1951 and the initial operational missions were usually flown with the reconnaissance aircraft as the lead in a four-ship flight of F-86 fighters. During 1951, the conversion of six more F-86As to reconnaissance configuration was authorised under Project Ashtray. In these Sabres, the available space below the cockpit was enlarged and fitted with constant temperature air conditioning for a forward oblique 24in K-11 camera and two 20in K-24 cameras mounted lengthwise with a mirror arrangement to provide vertical coverage. The Ashtray aircraft was officially designated as the RF-86A, distinguished from the fighter version by the presence of a pair of camera bay fairing bulges underneath the forward fuselage, just ahead of the wings. Some aircraft had an additional K-14 camera installed in the upper

F-86E 51-2832 was named *Karen's Kart* whilst assigned to the 51st Fighter Wing at Suwon Air Base in South Korea. The unit's markings are applied to the aircraft's tail fin and because it was flown by the wing's commanding officer, a multi-coloured band is painted on the nose section, denoting the three component squadrons of the 51st FW. ***(Photo: USAF)***

F-86A-5-NA 49-1096 was one of a batch of Sabres allocated to the Kentucky Air National Guard early in 1953, assigned to the fighter-bomber role as part of Tactical Air Command. *(Photo: USAF)*

After the Korean War, Sabres became the cornerstone of the US Air National Guard force. The ANG staged an annual cross-country air race, the Earl T. Ricks Memorial Trophy Race, and during the first competition in 1954, F-86E *Blackpool Bat IV* crashed during preparations for the event. *(Photo: USAF)*

forward part of the nose in place of the APG-30 radar, and some had open apertures for the cameras, while others had sliding doors that opened only when the cameras were in use. Most RF-86As were unarmed, although some retained the upper pair of 0.50in machine guns with limited ammunition. Despite being an effective reconnaissance system, the photos taken were often blurred due to vibration. A modified mirror installation helped to solve the vibration problem, but the slow-speed cameras continued to cause problems until they were replaced by a higher-speed K-14 system. During 1953, several F-86F-30s were fitted with reconnaissance cameras in Japan, under Project Haymaker. These conversions were similar to the Project Ashtray RF-86As, but with K-14 cameras in place of the lower-speed K-9s. The modified aircraft were re-designated as the RF-86F-30. Joining the 15th TRS at Kimpo in 1953, a small number of factory-built RF-86Fs began to appear in June 1953. These were equipped with two K-22 cameras and one K-17 camera inside a modified lower fuselage position. The cameras were mounted vertically, which took the main body of the camera and the film magazines outside of the fuselage contours, resulting in a bulge over the gun bay doors. Some 750lb of ballast was added to the forward fuselage to re-balance the aircraft's centre of gravity. A new elongated canopy was designed to counter an airflow buffet problem caused by the bulged fuselage, but by the time that these aircraft were ready for service, the Korean War had ended, although the RF-86F continued to perform reconnaissance missions in the region after the conflict concluded. ❖

BIGGER AND BETTER

North American Aviation develops the Sabre design still further

Man and machine. A USAF pilot next to his Sabre, F-86D-20-NA 51-2986. *(Photo: USAF)*

F-86H-10-NH Sabres with the Massachusetts Air National Guard, illustrating the familiar Sabre proportions, combined with the H-model's deeper fuselage. Included in the line-up is a visiting F-94C Starfire. *(Photo: USAF)*

North American Aviation's efforts to create a more capable Sabre resulted in the F-86F, with greater power from its engine and additional inboard weapons pylons. However, both the USAF and NAA accepted that the Sabre's design could be developed still further to produce an aircraft that was ideally suited to the fighter-bomber role, so that the USAF could employ the same aircraft either as an air superiority fighter or as a close-support bomber, depending on operational requirements. Design work on what eventually became the final version of the basic F-86 design (often referred to as the 'Sport Model') began in March 1951 as the NA-187, and by July a wooden mock-up of the new variant had been produced. It was built around the General Electric J73 engine, which promised to deliver at least 8,000lb thrust, representing roughly twice the power that had been available to the F-86 prototype. But to accommodate this engine's increased airflow requirements, the aircraft's air intake had to be widened, and this required a complete re-design of the fuselage structure, deepening the profile by some six inches. The re-shaped fuselage provided additional internal space, enabling fuel capacity to be increased from 435gal to 562gal, whilst retaining the same ability to carry up to four fuel tanks under the wings. NAA proposed that the new Sabre variant should be fitted with 20mm cannon, largely as a result of trials that had been performed in Korea. The MiG-15 proved to be a remarkably robust machine and many attacks performed by Sabre pilots were frustrated by an inability to cause sufficient damage to the MiGs that they intercepted. The 0.50in guns fitted to the Sabre simply didn't pack enough punch. Four F-86E-10s (51-2803, 2819, 2826 and 2836) and six F-86F-1s (51-2855, 2861, 2867, 2868, 2884 and 2900) were taken from the North American assembly line, fitted with four T-160 20mm cannon and re-designated as the F-86F-2-NA. The T-160 guns were belt-fed and were capable of firing 1,500 rounds per minute. The gun bays were redesigned with the guns spaced further apart vertically, combined with a totally new blast panel. The ammunition canisters could carry only 100 rounds, for approximately six seconds of firing. Tests were conducted in California and from Eglin AFB under Project Gunval, but major problems were encountered because of gun gas exhaust ingestion, which often caused engine flameouts. However the problems were eventually solved and the modified aircraft flew 242 combat missions in Korea, before they were finally returned to the USA. Encouraged by Project Gunval, the same 20mm cannon was to be installed in the NA-187, but development of this gun was still hampered by delays and the tried and tested 0.50in machine gun was reluctantly substituted, and eventually fitted to the first 115 production aircraft. Other modifications to the Sabre design included a revised

F-86H-10-NA 53-1298 was assigned to the 175th TFG, Maryland Air National Guard before being transferred to the Connecticut ANG a few years later, where it was painted in 'SE Asia' camouflage colours. It remained in service until June 1970 when it was withdrawn from use. Currently it is preserved and on display in Indiana. *(Photo: Key Collection)*

Many F-86H Sabres were painted in disruptive camouflage colours, as illustrated by F-86H-10-NA 53-1519, with the 138th TFS, New York ANG. This aircraft is still with 'The Boys from Syracuse' and is on display at Syracuse Airport. *(Photo: USAF)*

canopy shape and a more capable ejection seat, and re-designed elevators with no dihedral and increased area. Although armament options remained much the same as for the F-86F, the new variant was also equipped to carry a single Mk.12 20-kiloton nuclear bomb, which could be delivered using the then-new Low Altitude Bombing System (LABS) computer that had also been fitted to the F-86F.

Contract AF-27681 was issued on 3 November 1952 for 175 aircraft, designated as the F-86H-1. Two pre-production machines and a static test airframe would be built at Inglewood, while the rest would be manufactured at Columbus. The first machine (52-1975) completed its maiden flight on 30 April 1953 and deliveries to the USAF began early in 1954. Although the first aircraft to be completed were unmodified, the Columbus production line swiftly switched to the improved '6-3' wing (without wing slats) beginning with 52-1991, and also adopted a 12in wing tip extension that had first been introduced on the F-86F-40. The F-86H began to enter operational service in November 1954 when the 312th FBW at Clovis AFB received its first aircraft, followed by the 3595th CCTW at Nellis AFB. F-86H 52-2090 (the 115th aircraft) was the first to incorporate the planned T-160 cannon, now known as the M-39. This fearsome weapon effectively turned the aircraft into what became the 'definitive' expression of the original Sabre design, the F-86H-5. In June 1953 a contract (AF-22305) for a further 300 aircraft was issued. Although most of these F-86H-10s were essentially similar to earlier production batches, the final ten aircraft saw the re-introduction of the slatted wing, the USAF having concluded that as a versatile fighter-bomber, the additional speed and agility afforded by the '6-3' wing was unnecessary, and the better low-speed (particularly landing) characteristics of the slatted wing were preferable. Eventually, most F-86Hs were retrofitted with slatted wings. The USAF employed the F-86H for only a relatively short period, as by 1956 a new generation of aircraft was about to enter into service, not least the F-100 Super Sabre that joined the 312th FBW that year, replacing its F-86Hs. Many F-86Hs were deployed to Europe, and a considerable number went to the Air Force Reserve, before being

F-86H Sabres with the 101st FIS (102nd TFW) Massachusetts Air National Guard, on the ramp at their home base, Logan (Boston) Airport wearing the unit's distinctive green and white markings. *(Photo: USAF)*

withdrawn by the end of 1957. However, the F-86H became a significant part of the Air National Guard's inventory, remaining in use with various ANG units until the late 1960s, the very last Sabre mission occurring on 4 August 1970 when the 104th TFS flew F-86H 53-1370 to Seymour Johnson AFB for preservation. However, even this event was not the end of the USAF's Sabres as many aircraft continued to fly elsewhere, not least with the US Navy, where the aircraft became a valuable 'aggressor' training aircraft and an unmanned drone for armament trials.

While development of the F-86A had ultimately led to the 'definitive' F-86H, North American Aviation had also been pursuing other projects that were based on the same design, most notably the creation of an all-weather interceptor. The USAF had become increasingly worried by the risk of attack from Soviet strategic bombers that now possessed the capacity to reach across the Arctic Circle and strike directly at the continental USA. Great efforts were made to establish a more effective air defence system and as part of these efforts, various aircraft were brought into service, including the F-82 Twin Mustang and F-94 Starfire. Most of the projects were ultimately abandoned (usually because of commitments to other programmes) but when the preferred F-89 Scorpion also ran into delays, North American Aviation believed that the time was right to

Although initially assigned to the District of Columbia Air National Guard (as illustrated) F-86H-10-NA 53-1348 moved to the 121st FIS, Maryland ANG. The aircraft completed its USAF service with that unit and remains on display at Hyde Airport. *(Photo: USAF)*

pursue an all-weather interceptor design based on its F-86, under the company designation NA-164. Work on this project began in March 1949 and the USAF expressed great interest in it from the outset, even though NAA's proposed aircraft was very different from the many others that had been considered, chiefly because it was a single-seat machine. Equipped with Westinghouse AN/APG-36 radar and a Hughes E-3 Fire Control System (eventually switching to the E-4 system), the pilot would perform interceptions by radar, using a cathode ray tube screen fitted below the main instrument panel, thereby rendering a second crew member unnecessary. The more capable E-4 FCS would enable the aircraft to attack from any angle or direction, and most of the interception would be achieved automatically, reducing the need to rely on the interception skills of the pilot. The installation of the new radar system required a fairly drastic change

Prototype YF-86H-1-NA at Edwards AFB at the start of its test programme, having made its first flight on 30 April 1953. Ironically, despite having struggled to dissuade the media from calling the F-86 Sabre the 'Sabre Jet' for some time, the latter title was evidently applied to the YF-86H when it was first photographed. ***(Photo: Key Collection)***

A trio of F-86H Sabres from the 121st Fighter Squadron, District of Columbia Air National Guard, based at Andrews AFB. ***(Photo: USAF)***

to the Sabre's existing design, with the engine air intake being shifted downwards, to enable a large nose radome to be positioned ahead of the cockpit. The canopy design was changed to a 'clamshell' design, but in all other respects the aircraft remained similar to the F-86A, although the tail plane was eventually changed to a similar standard to that applied to the F-86H. The same four weapons or fuel pylons were retained and internal fuel capacity rose to 608gal. Consideration was given to the retention of the same 20mm cannon that was installed in late-model F-86Hs but by February 1950 this concept had been dropped in favour of 2.75in rocket projectiles, 24 of which would be carried inside a retractable tray fitted under the forward fuselage. Not surprisingly the NA-165 (designated as the F-86D for the USAF) was substantially heavier than its Sabre counterparts, but NAA adopted the more powerful J47-GE-17 engine rated at 6,650lb thrust, courtesy of a reheat system. This needed a slightly longer engine exhaust, requiring the F-86D fuselage to be stretched rearwards. Unfortunately for NAA, the modifications to the airframe were only part of the problems caused by the engine, as an electronic fuel control system was also introduced that became unreliable and troublesome, and remained problematical even as the aircraft entered service. Surprisingly, the rocket projectile armament system proved to be less of an issue. Based on the unguided R4M used by the wartime Messerschmitt Me 262, the 18lb folding fin

This close-up look at F-86H *Little Miss Mary* from the Maryland ANG shows the wing slat actuator mechanism clearly, as the Sabre's pilot (Col. Scott) signs to accept the aircraft prior to embarking on a mission. *(Photo: USAF)*

A rare photograph of the YF-86H prototype during early test flying from Edwards AFB. It is temporarily fitted with a long instrumentation boom ahead of the cockpit. *(Photo: USAF)*

'Mighty Mouse' rocket could be fired in salvos of six, twelve or 24, spreading outwards to give a shotgun effect with the same explosive power as a 75mm artillery shell. Impressive in theory, testing of the rockets demonstrated that only a full salvo of 24 rockets would be sufficiently accurate and lethal to destroy a target, and still only with a 60 per cent probability of success. But in this respect the rockets were probably no less reliable than the cannon or machine gun armament that was fitted to other Sabres.

Contract AF-9211 was issued on 7 October 1949 for 122 NA-165 aircraft and two NA-164 prototypes, equating to the F-86D and YF-86D in USAF parlance. However the USAF then re-designated the aircraft as the F-95A, on the basis that it was in effect a completely different machine to the existing Sabre family, sharing only 25 per cent parts commonality. Although this was true, it ignored the fact that some of these parts were pretty big (such as the wings and tail), and despite the design 'tweaks' the NA-165 was still undoubtedly a Sabre. Politics intervened, and NAA pressed for the reintroduction of the original designation, as Congress would need to approve funding for a completely new aircraft type. As a derivative of an existing design (rather than a completely new one), the F-86D would require rather less attention from those who held the purse strings. Thus, the F-95A eventually became the F-86D again, and the first aircraft (50-577) was completed at Inglewood in September 1949. It was transported to Muroc by road and made its first flight on 27 December in the hands of test pilot George Welch. Both this and the second prototype were modified quite extensively during the ensuing test programme, not least in terms of the rear fuselage structure, which was revised in accordance with changes in the engine afterburner design. Many other aspects were also investigated and although most did not translate into production changes for the F-86D, they were influential in the design of the F-100 Super Sabre that followed. The first F-86D-1 (50-455) took to the air on 8 June 1951. It was swiftly modified with vortex generators attached to parts of the fuselage and tail planes but in all other respects it was already representative of the production-standard airframe, boasting a top speed of 614 knots and a service ceiling of 55,400ft. Despite being 2,400lb heavier than the F-86A it possessed a climb rate of some 17,750ft/min – double that of the F-86A. Contract AF-19056 was issued on 11 April 1951 for a further 188 NA-17s, followed by another (AF-14800) on 18 July for 638 NA-173s. Yet another followed on 6 March 1952 (AF-6202) for a staggering total of 901 NA-190 airframes, reflecting the USAF's fears that defence of the US mainland was woefully inadequate, given the circumstances of the conflict that was taking place in Korea. During this same month the USAF took delivery of its first F-86D (50-560) at Edwards AFB, and by July the 3625th Flying Training Wing at Tyndall AFB had begun crew training on the type. However, introduction of the F-86D into USAF service was slow, partly because of developmental delays, but also due to many problems caused by the introduction of so many systems. In an era when transistors and solid-state electronics were still new, the F-86D was a sophisticated aircraft, and countless issues arose where

During 1947 North American Aviation began design study NA-157 to create a 'penetration fighter' to meet the requirements that had been set out by the USAF for a long-range version of the F-86A. In order to accommodate more fuel, a much larger Sabre was envisioned, able to carry 1,961 US gallons of fuel both internally and with two underwing drop tanks. The new variant possessed an unrefuelled range of more than 2,000nm, and the resultant fighter design was designated as the F-86C. The new aircraft was much larger and heavier, weighing in at 10,640lb more than the F-86A. The increased weight and size necessitated a dual-wheel main landing gear, increased wing area and a more powerful engine, in the shape of a Pratt & Whitney J48 rated at 6,250lb thrust (8,750lb with afterburner). With SCR-720 search radar and six 20mm cannon, the new design replaced the Sabre's single air intake with flush-mounted NACA inlets either side of the fuselage. The USAF ordered two prototype NA-157s and in view of the aircraft's considerable changes, re-designated it as the YF-93A. The first prototype was built with the NACA inlet ducts but following problems with the design, the second aircraft was completed with more conventional intakes. Six months later, the initial contract was followed by an order for 118 F-93A-NAs. However, in 1949 the order was cancelled, primarily because of the emergence of faster bomber designs such as the B-47 that would not need fighter escort. The two prototypes were transferred to NACA (NASA) and used for experimental duties until 1956.
(Photos: Key Collection)

USAF

The second YF-86D (50-578) was assigned to Hughes Aircraft for radar trials before being delivered to the USAF in March 1952. It was subsequently transferred to NACA for further flight testing. *(Photo: Key Collection)*

YF-86D-NA (YF-95A) 50-577 some weeks after its first flight on 27 December 1949. By this time the aircraft was being employed on initial weapon release trials. *(Photo: NAA)*

An F-86D performing for the camera in flamboyant style during 1954. F-86D-30-NA 51-6143 was assigned to the 575th Air Defense Group, based at Selfridge AFB in Michigan. ***(Photo: USAF)***

incorrect wiring or wrongly installed systems caused quality control delays. The last F-86D-1 was not delivered to the USAF until October 1952, some three years after the contract had been issued. These aircraft were assigned to either test or training duties, the E-3 FCS being of only limited operational use. A number had their radar and armament equipment removed (replaced by ballast) and were then used as high-speed pacer aircraft deployed as chase planes for pilot conversion training, designated as the TF-86D. It wasn't until Block 15 aircraft became available that deliveries to operational units began, starting with the 94th FIS at George AFB in February 1953. The 325rd FIS at Larson AFB duly re-equipped in April, followed by the 62nd FIS at O'Hare, the 95th FIS at Andrews AFB and the 60th FIS at Westover AFB.

As a relatively complex aircraft, the F-86D required greater pilot training than necessary for other Sabre variants, and this was reflected in a larger USAF training network. Although its complexity didn't increase significantly, the aircraft's basic configuration was progressively modified, to incorporate various aerodynamic, engine and system modifications as they became available. For example, a powered rudder was fitted, a single-point refuelling system, relocated external power system receptacles (enabling the aircraft to operate from 'alert barns'), and jettisonable drop tanks. This process continued, and the J47 engine was gradually improved to deliver 7,650lb thrust with reheat, while from the F-86D-45 batch onwards, all aircraft were modified to carry a braking parachute in a redesigned tail fairing under the rudder, enabling the type to land more comfortably on shorter runways. The result of these many changes was that the huge Sabre fleet comprised many aircraft completed to very different standards, creating a logistical nightmare for

F-86D-40-NA 52-3760, resplendent in the markings of the 173rd Fighter Interceptor Squadron, Nebraska Air National Guard. The aircraft was retained by the Nebraska ANG after retirement and remains on display at Lincoln. *(Photo: USAF)*

ANG
ANG-760

F-86D-50-NA 52-4274 was converted to F-86L standard and re-assigned to the 187th Fighter Interceptor Squadron, Wyoming Air National Guard. As can be seen, the 'US Air Force' titling was removed from the fuselage during the conversion process. *(Photo: USAF)*

maintenance units. Late in 1953 the USAF initiated Project Pullout, in which the F-86Ds were modified to a single F-86D-45 standard, aircraft being rotated through NAA's Fresno site, or the USAF's McClellan AFB Sacramento Air Material Area facility.

By 1955 most of the F-86D Sabre fleet had been modified to a common standard, apart from a small number of very early machines that were not put through the programme. This enabled the USAF to begin deploying the aircraft to Europe, although pilots who were already accustomed to derivatives of the standard day fighter version were reluctant to embrace the F-86D. The 'Sabre Dog' was certainly not as manoeuvrable as its Sabre siblings, and the F-86D was often regarded as a rather cumbersome radar interceptor, very different to the more glamorous MiG killers, and the F-86E. But with time USAF pilots began to appreciate the capabilities of the all-weather interceptor, which performed well and suffered from very few vices. Indeed, the only serious difficulty that was never fully resolved was the temperamental nature of the engine's electronic fuel control system. F-86Ds re-equipped squadrons in Germany, France, Britain, Morocco and Libya, and early in 1954 the first examples arrived in Japan, where the F-86 remained for many years, while the delicate relationship between the US, Taiwan, North and South Korea went through many twists and turns. It wasn't until November 1958 that the last FEAF Sabre deployment ended.

On 12 June 1953 a final contract (AF-22303) was placed for 624 machines, designated as NA-201 (F-86D-55 and F-86D-60). These were mostly assigned to Air Defense Command units in order to upgrade the fleet of available interceptors. The J47-GE-33 fitted in the final 987 F-86Ds was more powerful than the engine fitted to earlier aircraft. The J47-GE-33's static thrust with afterburner reached 7,650lb and featured better cooling and afterburner ignition. This batch of aircraft was to have been designated as the F-86G but the proposal was dropped and that designation was never applied to any operational Sabres. The F-86K was an export version of the all-weather interceptor (as described later), while the F-86L was a modified variant of the

Pictured in typical USAF markings comprising unpainted metal finish with fluorescent orange trim, F-86D-40-NA 52-3719 with the 151st FIS, Tennessee ANG, at Knoxville during 1959. The aircraft was withdrawn just a few months later and is now preserved in Ohio. *(Photo: USAF)*

Baking under the Texas sun, F-86D-40-NA 52-3725 with the 181st FIS, Texas ANG. This aircraft had previously served with the 14th FIS and 85th FIS, and remained in use until April 1960 when it was flown to Davis Monthan AFB for long-term storage. *(Photo: USAF)*

aircraft, equipped to function with SAGE (Semi Automatic Ground Environment) equipment. SAGE was designed to replace the less-than perfect USAF Ground Control Intercept system in which ground controllers verbally relayed intercept information to the Sabre pilot, based on their radar information. In order to speed up the process, a new arrangement of GCI sites would transmit radar data electronically to the aircraft in real time, so that the pilot could steer an automatic course onto his target. SAGE was a sound concept but it took years to perfect the system, although the decision to modify aircraft to employ SAGE (Project Follow On) also enabled NAA to improve other aspects of the F-86D, not least by installing '6-3' slatted wings and the 12in wing tip extension, creating what was referred-to as the 'F-40' wing configuration. Externally, the F-86L was also distinguishable from the F-86D through the replacement of unsatisfactory NACA engine cooling inlets on the fuselage with more conventional 'sugar scoop' intakes, although these were also retrofitted to some F-86Ds. The first F-86L made its maiden flight late in 1955, entering USAF service the following year, and eventually some 981 aircraft were modified to F-86L standard, equipping both frontline squadrons and training units. When the new F-102 and F-106 interceptors started to enter USAF service, most of the F-86D and F-86L fleet was progressively transferred to the Air National Guard, the first ANG unit to re-equip being the 173rd FIS (Nebraska ANG) during May 1957. They remained in use for some time, but as the F-102 Delta Dagger became available, the ANG also relinquished its Sabres, and the last such unit to operate the type (the 196th FIS, California ANG) relinquished them in the summer of 1965.

The story of the United States Air Force's association with the Sabre is certainly well-known, but the United States Navy's adoption of the aircraft is often overlooked, even though the Sabre owed its origins to the US Navy. As described previously, it was the creation of the NA-134 that led to the development of the XP-86 for the USAF, and this swept-wing variant of the original NA-134 went on to become the basis of the many Sabre derivatives that followed. But while the USAF pursued the swept-wing

F-86D-55-NA 53-666 at Hensley Field whilst serving with the 181st FIS, Texas ANG. After conversion to F-86L standard, the aircraft was transferred to the 187th FIS, Wyoming ANG. *(Photo: USAF)*

Although the F-86D was primarily assigned to USAF units based in the US, a considerable number were also deployed to Europe, as illustrated by this aircraft from the 526th FIS, 86th TFW, based at Bitburg AB in Germany. ***(Photo: USAF)***

Pictured in October 1956, F-86D-30-NA 51-5986 was transferred to NACA for experimental duties, and (as illustrated) achieved the 3,000th hour on jet aircraft that the NACA Ames research facility. It was subsequently transferred to the JASDF as 84-8134 and is now preserved at Matsushima Air Base in Japan. ***(Photo: NASA)***

XP-86, the US Navy's chiefs steadfastly stuck with their decision to acquire the straight-winged aircraft that had been designed for them by NAA. Three NA-135 prototypes were ordered on 1 January 1945 and from the outset these aircraft were very different to the XP-86 that NAA designed for the USAF. The NA-135 did of course have straight wings, and this was largely because the Navy's primary interest was the low-speed reliability and safety that was vital for carrier operations. Unusually, a wing folding mechanism was not adopted because the wing-mounted dive brakes would have made wing folding difficult to achieve. Instead, NAA designed an unusual 'kneeling' nose wheel assembly that enabled the aircraft to be stacked tightly inside a carrier deck in a tail-high position. The fuselage bore some resemblance to the XP-86 but was far less streamlined and incorporated a large dorsal access panel to allow the J35 engine to be removed, contrasting with the simpler one-piece tail assembly designed for the XP-86. The first XFJ-1 made its maiden flight on 11 September 1946, in the hands of test pilot Wallace Lien. By the end of February 1947 all three prototypes were flying. In May 1945 the US Navy had issued contract Noa(S)6911 for 100 FJ-1s, although only 30 were ultimately produced, the last example being delivered to the Navy just a few weeks before the first P-86A was delivered to the USAF. VF-5A at NAS North Island was the only squadron to acquire the FJ-1, the first aircraft arriving on 15 November 1947. Tasked with the evaluation of the aircraft at sea, the initial FJ-1 carrier landing was made on 16 March 1948 (on USS *Boxer*), followed by the first launch, although with relatively poor engine power and acceleration, all further launches were made by catapult. By this stage the aircraft had become known as the Fury, although there is little evidence to establish how and when this name was chosen. VF-5A eventually became VF-51 and with a fleet of 24 aircraft, the unit enjoyed a successful relationship with the FJ-1, despite some accidents. The aircraft performed adequately, although it was hampered by a weak undercarriage that was less than ideal for carrier operations, and when the new F9F-3 Panther became available the unremarkable FJ-1 was withdrawn in May 1949. The Fury was transferred to Naval Air Reserve units, the

F-86D-50-NA 52-470, assigned to the 199th Fighter Interceptor Squadron, Hawaii Air National Guard, at Hickam AFB. *(Photo: USAF)*

last example being withdrawn from use in July 1953.

By this stage the US Navy had of course turned its attention to the far greater potential of the swept-wing Sabre. NAA started work on a swept-wing Fury design in January 1951, the NA-181 becoming what was in effect a 'navalised' version of the F-86E. NAA proposed this to the US Navy on 6 February and just four days later the Navy eagerly ordered 300 examples, although this number was eventually reduced to 200 because of Korean War production issues. Two pre-production NA-179 aircraft (designated as the XFJ-2) were also ordered, together with a single NA-185 (XFJ-2B), these being based on production F-86E-10 airframes, but with a modified undercarriage — made considerably stronger and with a raised nose wheel leg — and a tail hook. They were also designed to carry a 200gal drop tank that would be common to all production machines. Although the two XFJ-2 aircraft were unarmed, the XFJ-2B was used to test the armament system and didn't feature the other naval modifications. Four Colt Mk.12 20mm cannon were selected, each with 150 rounds, positioned in the same forward fuselage positions as had been designed for the F-86E. The XFJ-2B took to the air on 27 December 1951, piloted by Bob Hoover. This was followed by the first XFJ-2 on 14 February 1952, and by the end of that year the aircraft was being tested at sea. Unfortunately the new landing gear proved to be inadequate for carrier recoveries, and the aircraft's handling on approach and landing was poor. But with production already under way, these deficiencies were accepted and the aircraft was delivered to the Navy with these issues still unresolved. Externally similar to the F-86E, the FJ-2 was primarily distinguished from its USAF counterpart by the addition of the arrester hook and tail skid, and with an extended nose wheel leg, the aircraft appeared markedly different when on the ground. Wing folding was incorporated into the design, and as a result of this the wing's leading edge was divided into two portions, operating as two separate panels in much the same way as the original XP-86 had done. The 6,000lb-thrust J47-GE-2 (a naval derivative of the J47-GE-13) was adopted on production aircraft, and ammunition capacity

F-86D-40-NA 52-3630 was modified to become the prototype YF-86K. It was operated by North American Aviation on test duties until 1960 when it was placed in storage at Davis Monthan AFB, being scrapped there in 1961. *(Photo: NAA)*

was increased to 720 rounds in total, using an AN/APG-30 and Mk.16 gun sight system. Tail plane dihedral was abandoned, and the cockpit windshield was repositioned to provide better forward view for the pilot. A British Martin-Baker ejection seat was chosen, which resulted in a redesigned canopy.

Production of the FJ-2 (all performed at Columbus) was slowed by the need to allocate resources to Korean War work, and by January 1954 only 25 aircraft had been delivered to the Navy, but with production of the F-86F at an end, the Columbus factory then shifted its resources towards the FJ-2 and the last had been delivered by September. The aircraft were all assigned to US Marine Corps units, as it had been planned to equip the USMC with the aircraft for operations in Korea. Despite the production delays that had prevented the FJ-2 from reaching Korea, the aircraft still went to the Marines. VMF-122 at Cherry Point received the first aircraft in January 1954, while VMF-235 at El Toro did so before deploying on board the USS *Hancock* in June. The FJ-2 Fury performed adequately, but as expected it suffered from the same carrier deficiencies that had affected the pre-production aircraft. Even more unsatisfactory was the aircraft's poor combat performance, due to a wholly unsuitable cannon aiming arrangement whereby NAA had aligned the cannon's muzzle axis below the aircraft's longitudinal axis. It had been thought that this would improve aiming in high g conditions but in practise it had precisely the opposite effect. It was hardly surprising therefore that the FJ-2 Fury enjoyed only a brief spell of operational service with the USMC, and by the end of 1956 the aircraft had been withdrawn, the majority moving to Naval Reserve units for a few months, before being retired. NAA's attempts to improve the FJ-2 had included investigations into the use of the non-slatted '6-3' wing, as this would have improved the aircraft's speed and manoeuvrability. However, it would have decreased the already poor low-speed characteristics still further, so an alternative proposal was investigated, using a full-chord wing fence attached to a non-slatted '6-3' wing, combined with 12in wing tip extensions. It resulted in potentially dangerous roll, yaw and stall tendencies, and various wing fence designs and positions were tested in order to find an arrangement that cured these problems. Eventually, wing fences across the leading edges at stations 100 and 176 were found to provide the best solution, but by this stage it was too late to incorporate these modifications into the FJ-2, so the knowledge that had been gleaned was carried to the next variant, the FJ-3 (NA-194). Work on this project began in March 1952 in an attempt to produce an aircraft with better performance and payload, built around a licence-produced version of the British Armstrong Siddeley Sapphire engine, the Wright J65-W-4, ultimately rated at 7,650lb thrust. No prototype was ordered, but the fifth FJ-2 was refitted with the J65 engine (as the NA-196) and this aircraft made its first flight from Columbus on 3 July 1953. For production aircraft, the air intake was enlarged to provide greater mass flow for the engine, and the larger forward fuselage enabled an additional 48 rounds of cannon ammunition to be carried. The first production aircraft made its maiden flight on 1 December 1953 and VF-173 at Jacksonville

A United States Navy Landing Signal Officer (LSO) guides an FJ-2 Fury towards the runway during field carrier landing practice in 1954. *(Photo: US Navy)*

▲► **XFJ-2 prototype 133754 made its first flight on 14 February 1952 before being assigned to the Naval Air Test Center (NATC) at Patuxent River. The aircraft spent some time on board the USS *Coral Sea* for carrier trials and remained in use with the NATC until 1955 when it was assigned to ground instructional duties at NAMC, Philadelphia.** ***(Photos: US Navy)***

became the first squadron to operate the aircraft, from September 1954. Sadly, many of the FJ-2's deficiencies were carried over to the FJ-3, not least the less-than-ideal carrier performance and the poor cannon aiming, exacerbated by further problems surrounding the J65 engine that suffered from turbine blade failures and a tendency to seize during catapult launches. Further attention was given to the wing design, and a number of early FJ-3s featured five small leading-edge fences across their wings, that improved low-speed handling. Attention then returned to the '6-3' wing, and NAA eventually produced a new leading-edge extension design that featured a cambered surface, based on NACA research. It promised to solve the handling problems and also provided additional space for additional fuel. However, it required a great deal of testing and evaluation, so a simpler 'fix' was devised in which four of the existing small wing fences were retained, and combined with a new, larger fence just outboard of the wing fold. From July 1955 this wing modification was introduced into production and progressively retrofitted to earlier aircraft. The only further change made to the FJ-3's wing was the installation of two additional pylons, enabling the outer stations to carry 200gal drop tanks, the inner pylons 500lb bombs (or rocket projectiles), and the middle stations being made available for either 1,000lb bombs or Sidewinder AAMs, these modified aircraft (from the 345th onwards) being re-designated as the FJ-3M. From 1 October 1962 the FJ-3 became the F-1C, as part of a new tri-service designation scheme. The earlier FJ-1 and FJ-2 were not given new

Two US Marine Corps FJ-2s from Marine Fighter Squadron VMF-235 during a mission from the unit's home base at MCAS El Toro in California in 1954. *(Photo: US Navy)*

A VMF-451 FJ-2 Fury on the flight line at MCAS El Toro during 1954. *(Photo: US Navy)*

designations (having been withdrawn), but the FJ-3M became the MF-3C. The FJ-3 could hardly be described as a hugely successful aircraft, but it proved to be sufficiently suitable for routine operational use and it remained in front-line service for some time, with many examples eventually being converted into drone director aircraft that supported the Vought Regulus missile programme and F6F-6K drone operations. These were duly designated as the DF-1C and DF-1D under the new system implemented in 1962.

Arguably the most capable and best of all the Sabre's many variants was the Navy's final version, the FJ-4 Fury. Despite drawing on the experience gained during the development of the FJ-2 and FJ-3, the FJ-4 was a very different machine that could arguably have been regarded as a completely new aircraft, even though it shared more than a superficial resemblance to earlier members of the Sabre family. Project NA-208 began in February 1953 in response to a Navy requirement for an aircraft to replace the cancelled McDonnell F3H Demon. Two prototypes were ordered in June and a contract for 43 NA-209 aircraft was issued on 16 October. The Navy's performance requirements stipulated that the FJ-4 should be at least as good as the F3H Demon or better, and this required drastic changes to the Sabre's design. Most significant was the range requirement, and this necessitated a 50 per cent increase in fuel capacity. The fuselage structure had to be completely redesigned, with a deeper profile and an extended dorsal spine, while a completely new wing was also developed. Retaining the standard 35-degree sweep angle, NAA's team sought a six per cent thickness-to-chord ratio with additional leading-edge camber that would create additional fuel capacity. The '6-3' wing that had been developed for the FJ-3 was used as the basis for a new design, combined with slotted trailing-edge flaps. It was feared that the new, highly tapered wing would cause tip stalling problems, but rigorous testing demonstrated that it was in fact extremely stable at all speeds. The Navy increased its order to 107 aircraft and the first FJ-4 completed its maiden flight at Columbus on 28 October 1954, piloted by Richard Wenzell. As expected, the aircraft performed well, although some directional instability was reported and this resulted in a modified tall fin of greater length. From the 33rd production example onwards, the Wright

▲▼ Rare images of early FJ-2 Furies assigned to the Naval Air Test Center at Patuxent River, Maryland. As can be seen, the Fury retained the basic proportions and contours of the F-86 Sabre but also incorporated some subtle changes, not least the re-shaped forward fuselage and cockpit canopy, re-designed external fuel tanks, and the longer (and stronger) landing gear. ***(Photos: US Navy)***

The first FJ-4 Fury emerges from North American Aviation's Columbus factory, 28 October 1954. *(Photo: NAA)*

FJ-4B 143585, assigned to VMA-212 on board the USS *Oriskany*, illustrating the larger wing layout of this Fury variant. The aircraft was withdrawn from use during 1964, at NAS Memphis. *(Photo: US Navy)*

(Photo: US Navy)

Pictured whilst assigned to the Naval Air Reserve Training Unit at Glenview, Illinois, FJ-4B 139531 is currently preserved and on display at the Pima Air and Space Museum in Arizona.

J65-W-16 engine was installed, delivering 7,700lb thrust. Earlier aircraft were progressively refitted with engines modified to this standard. Flight refuelling equipment (first applied to part of the FJ-3 fleet) was fitted as standard, and with its greatly improved performance, the US Marine Corps gleefully received its first aircraft in September 1956 when VMF-323 acquired its first examples. By March 1957 the entire fleet of 150 aircraft had been delivered.

A batch of 25 FJ-4Bs was ordered on 26 July 1954, these being developed from the standard FJ-4 airframe as a dedicated ground attack variant, the first example taking to the air on 3 December 1956. It incorporated a stronger wing structure, supporting six weapons pylons that could carry up to 6,000lb of fuel, rockets or bombs, including nuclear stores if necessary (a special pylon was designed for these, which could be fitted to the port wing). Additional speed brakes were mounted on the rear fuselage, designed to slow and stabilise speed for low-level attack profiles (they didn't operate when the undercarriage was lowered). A second order for some 46 aircraft (NA-299) was followed by a final order for 151 aircraft (the NA-244), placed on 5 April 1956. The last aircraft, bringing the total to 222, was delivered in May 1958. Although designed to carry a variety of stores, including the ASM-N-7 Bullpup air-to-surface guided missile (of which five could be carried), the FJ-4B was primarily assigned to the use of nuclear stores, using LABS delivery techniques. One aircraft was used to demonstrate the operational capability of this system, flying from Quonset Point to NAS Payport in Florida, from where its pilot delivered a dummy Mk.28 tactical nuclear bomb before returning to Rhode Island, thereby demonstrating a combat radius of some 820 nautical miles. Judged as a great success, the FJ-4B remained in use until January 1962, by which stage the A-4 Skyhawk had come into service, although the Fury remained active with reserve units until 1964, becoming the AF-1E from 1 October 1962. The FJ-4 duly became the F-1E. ❖

This FJ-3 Fury from VF-21 illustrates the wing fold mechanism devised for the Fury. The outboard wing section was designed to hinge inwards along the wing chord, at a point between the inboard flaps and outboard ailerons. *(Photo: US Navy)*

THE F-86 SABRE IN DETAIL

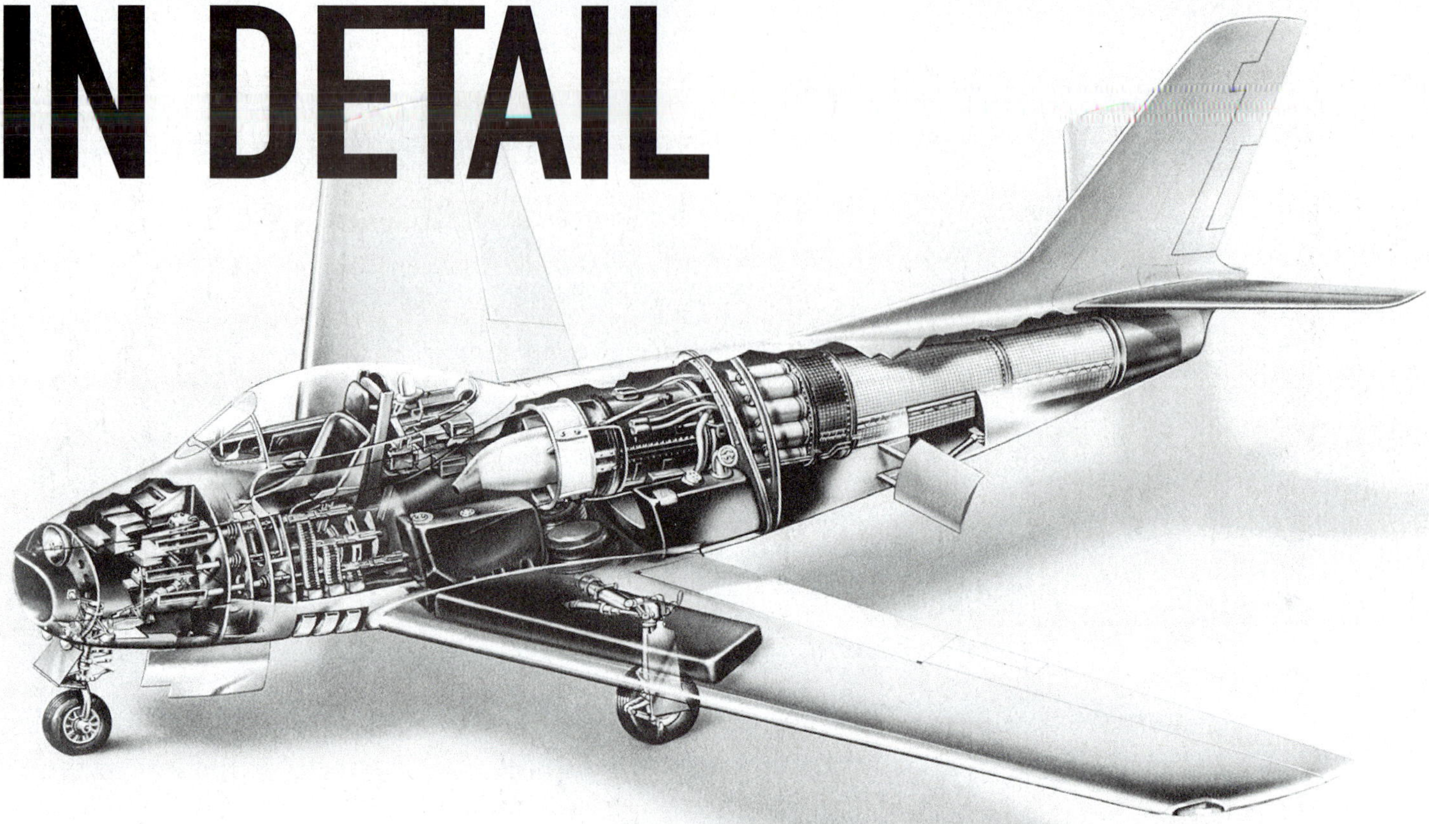

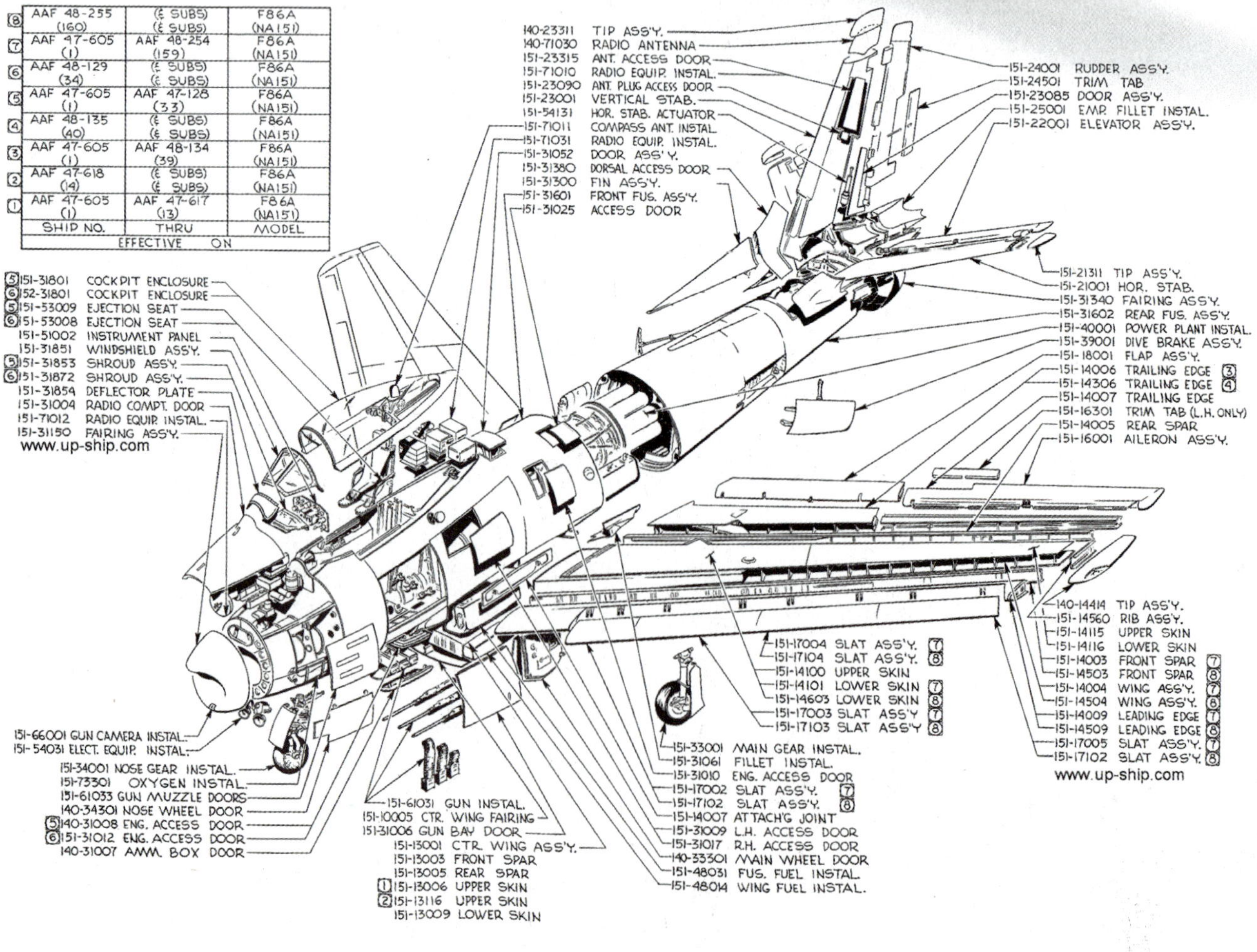

	SHIP NO.	THRU	MODEL
[8]	AAF 48-255 (160)	(& SUBS) (& SUBS)	F86A (NA151)
[7]	AAF 47-605 (1)	AAF 48-254 (159)	F86A (NA151)
[6]	AAF 48-129 (34)	(& SUBS) (& SUBS)	F86A (NA151)
[5]	AAF 47-605 (1)	AAF 47-128 (33)	F86A (NA151)
[4]	AAF 48-135 (40)	(& SUBS) (& SUBS)	F86A (NA151)
[3]	AAF 47-605 (1)	AAF 48-134 (39)	F86A (NA151)
[2]	AAF 47-618 (14)	(& SUBS) (& SUBS)	F86A (NA151)
[1]	AAF 47-605 (1)	AAF 47-617 (13)	F86A (NA151)
	EFFECTIVE ON		

140-23311 TIP ASS'Y.
140-71030 RADIO ANTENNA
151-23315 ANT. ACCESS DOOR
151-71010 RADIO EQUIP. INSTAL.
151-23090 ANT. PLUG ACCESS DOOR
151-23001 VERTICAL STAB.
151-54131 HOR. STAB. ACTUATOR
151-71011 COMPASS ANT. INSTAL.
151-71031 RADIO EQUIP. INSTAL.
151-31052 DOOR ASS'Y.
151-31380 DORSAL ACCESS DOOR
151-31300 FIN ASS'Y.
151-31601 FRONT FUS. ASS'Y.
151-31025 ACCESS DOOR

151-24001 RUDDER ASS'Y.
151-24501 TRIM TAB
151-23085 DOOR ASS'Y.
151-25001 EMP. FILLET INSTAL.
151-22001 ELEVATOR ASS'Y.

[5] 151-31801 COCKPIT ENCLOSURE
[6] 152-31801 COCKPIT ENCLOSURE
[5] 151-53009 EJECTION SEAT
[6] 151-53008 EJECTION SEAT
151-51002 INSTRUMENT PANEL
151-31851 WINDSHIELD ASS'Y.
[5] 151-31853 SHROUD ASS'Y.
[6] 151-31872 SHROUD ASS'Y.
151-31854 DEFLECTOR PLATE
151-31004 RADIO COMPT. DOOR
151-71012 RADIO EQUIP. INSTAL.
151-31150 FAIRING ASS'Y.
www.up-ship.com

151-21311 TIP ASS'Y.
151-21001 HOR. STAB.
151-31340 FAIRING ASS'Y.
151-31602 REAR FUS. ASS'Y.
151-40001 POWER PLANT INSTAL.
151-39001 DIVE BRAKE ASS'Y.
151-18001 FLAP ASS'Y.
151-14006 TRAILING EDGE [3]
151-14306 TRAILING EDGE [4]
151-14007 TRAILING EDGE
151-16301 TRIM TAB (L.H. ONLY)
151-14005 REAR SPAR
151-16001 AILERON ASS'Y.

140-14414 TIP ASS'Y.
151-14560 RIB ASS'Y.
151-14115 UPPER SKIN
151-14116 LOWER SKIN
151-14003 FRONT SPAR [7]
151-14503 FRONT SPAR [8]
151-14004 WING ASS'Y. [7]
151-14504 WING ASS'Y. [8]
151-14009 LEADING EDGE [7]
151-14509 LEADING EDGE [8]
151-17005 SLAT ASS'Y. [7]
151-17102 SLAT ASS'Y. [8]
www.up-ship.com

151-17004 SLAT ASS'Y. [7]
151-17104 SLAT ASS'Y. [8]
151-14100 UPPER SKIN
151-14101 LOWER SKIN [7]
151-14603 LOWER SKIN [8]
151-17003 SLAT ASS'Y [7]
151-17103 SLAT ASS'Y [8]

151-66001 GUN CAMERA INSTAL.
151-54031 ELECT. EQUIP. INSTAL.
151-34001 NOSE GEAR INSTAL.
151-73301 OXYGEN INSTAL.
151-61033 GUN MUZZLE DOORS
140-34301 NOSE WHEEL DOOR
[5] 140-31008 ENG. ACCESS DOOR
[6] 151-31012 ENG. ACCESS DOOR
140-31007 AMM. BOX DOOR

151-61031 GUN INSTAL.
151-10005 CTR. WING FAIRING
151-31006 GUN BAY DOOR
151-13001 CTR. WING ASS'Y.
151-13003 FRONT SPAR
151-13005 REAR SPAR
[1] 151-13006 UPPER SKIN
[2] 151-13116 UPPER SKIN
151-13009 LOWER SKIN

151-33001 MAIN GEAR INSTAL.
151-31061 FILLET INSTAL.
151-31010 ENG. ACCESS DOOR
151-17002 SLAT ASS'Y. [7]
151-17102 SLAT ASS'Y. [8]
151-14007 ATTACH'G JOINT
151-31009 L.H. ACCESS DOOR
151-31017 R.H. ACCESS DOOR
140-33301 MAIN WHEEL DOOR
151-48031 FUS. FUEL INSTAL.
151-48014 WING FUEL INSTAL.

SABRE F-86E

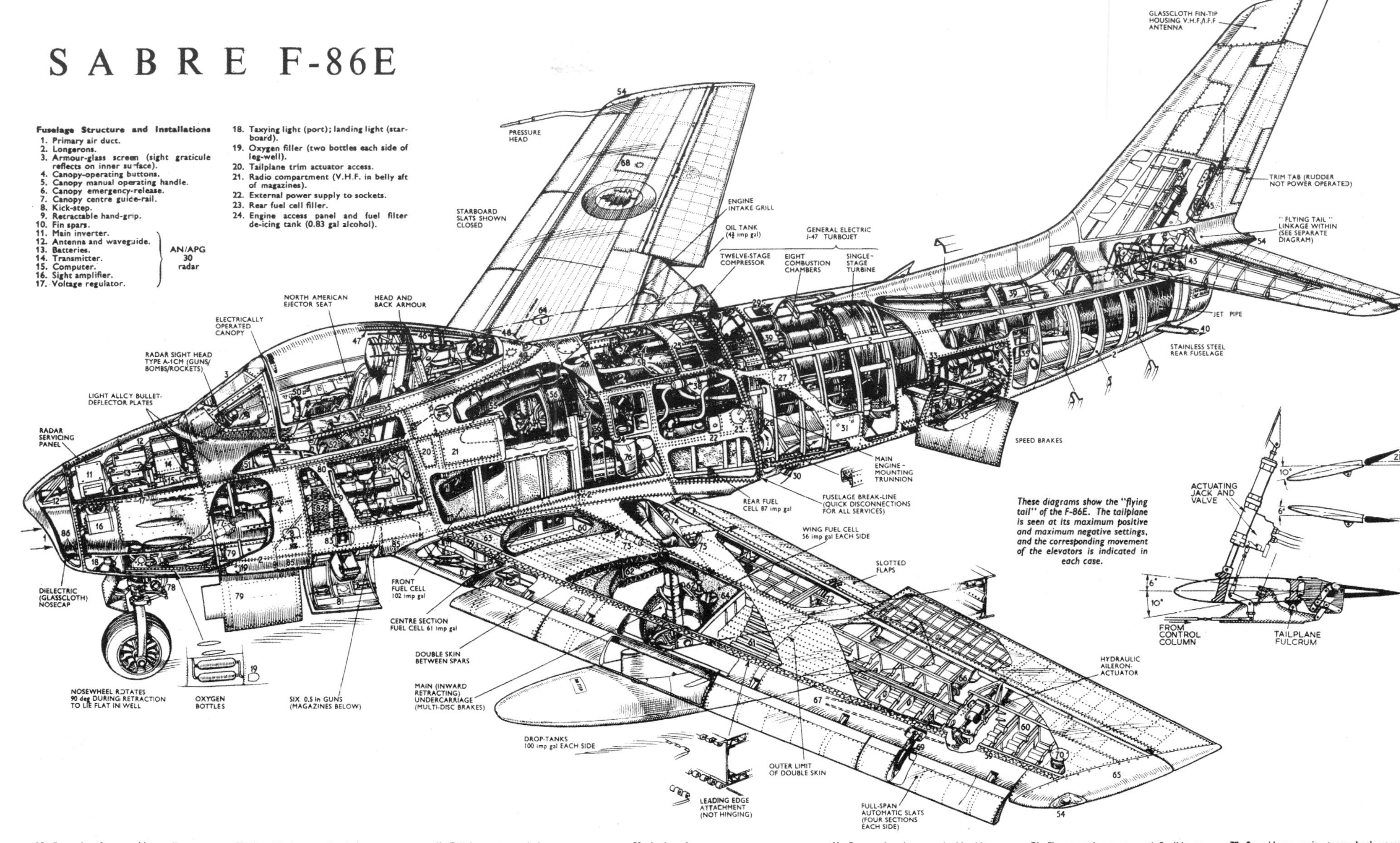

These diagrams show the "flying tail" of the F-86E. The tailplane is seen at its maximum positive and maximum negative settings, and the corresponding movement of the elevators is indicated in each case.

Fuselage Structure and Installations

1. Primary air duct.
2. Longerons.
3. Armour-glass screen (sight graticule reflects on inner surface).
4. Canopy-operating buttons.
5. Canopy manual operating handle.
6. Canopy emergency-release.
7. Canopy centre guide-rail.
8. Kick-step.
9. Retractable hand-grip.
10. Fin spars.
11. Main inverter.
12. Antenna and waveguide.
13. Batteries.
14. Transmitter.
15. Computer.
16. Sight amplifier.
17. Voltage regulator.

(11–17: AN/APG 30 radar)

18. Taxying light (port); landing light (starboard).
19. Oxygen filler (two bottles each side of leg-well).
20. Tailplane trim actuator access.
21. Radio compartment (V.H.F. in belly aft of magazines).
22. External power supply to sockets.
23. Rear fuel cell filler.
24. Engine access panel and fuel filter de-icing tank (0.83 gal alcohol).
25. Control-surface cable adjustment access.
26. Hot outlet from air-conditioning unit.
27. Igniter plug access.
28. Compressor section ventilation air intake.
29. Compressor section ventilation air outlet.
30. Rear fuselage ventilation air intake. ... data case;
32. Speed-brake actuating jack.
33. Emergency control reservoir.
34. Emergency hydraulic accumulator.
35. Power control compensator.
36. Power control normal accumulator.
37. Power control normal reservoir.
38. Heat exchanger (cockpit air-conditioning system).
39. Control-surface cable-duct.
42. Tailplane actuator jack.
43. Tailplane rear spar (hinged).
44. Rudder control quadrant.
45. Tab-actuating motor.
46. Radio compass (type ARN-6) loop antenna.
47. Radio compass sense antenna.
48. Cockpit pressure regulator and outlet.
49. Upward identification light.
50. Control column.
51. Port rudder-pedal.
52. Engine-power control.
53. Anti-g valve.
54. Navigation lights.

Engine

55. Nose cone (engine auxiliaries within).
56. Starter/generator.
57. Engine steady and guide-rail.
58. Ignition units.

Wing Structure and Installations

59. Front spar.
60. Rear spar.
61. Corrugations between double skin.
62. Constructional posts bolted through fuel cell.
63. Glasscloth liner (anti-chafe and bullet deflector).
64. Fuel fillers.
65. Moulded wing-tip.
66. Irving balanced ailerons.
67. Aileron control cables.
68. Aileron actuator access.
69. Slat roller and guide-rail assemblies.
70. Gyrosyn compass flux unit.
71. Flap actuating motor and flexible co-ordinating shaft.
72. Flap roller-and-guide-rail assemblies.

Undercarriage Units

73. Mainwheel operating jack.
74. Uplock cylinder.
75. Downlock cylinder.
76. Wheel-well with raised portion for brake drum.
77. Nosewheel operating jack (under air-duct).
78. Steer/damp unit (nosewheel steers 23 deg each side).
79. Nosewheel door and jack.

Armament

80. Gun access panel.
81. Magazine door/entry step.
82. Flexible belt-guides.
83. Feed boosters.
84. Gun-heating cables.
85. Spent case and link compartments.
86. Camera gun.

F-86A
erican
Sabre
F-86E
wing

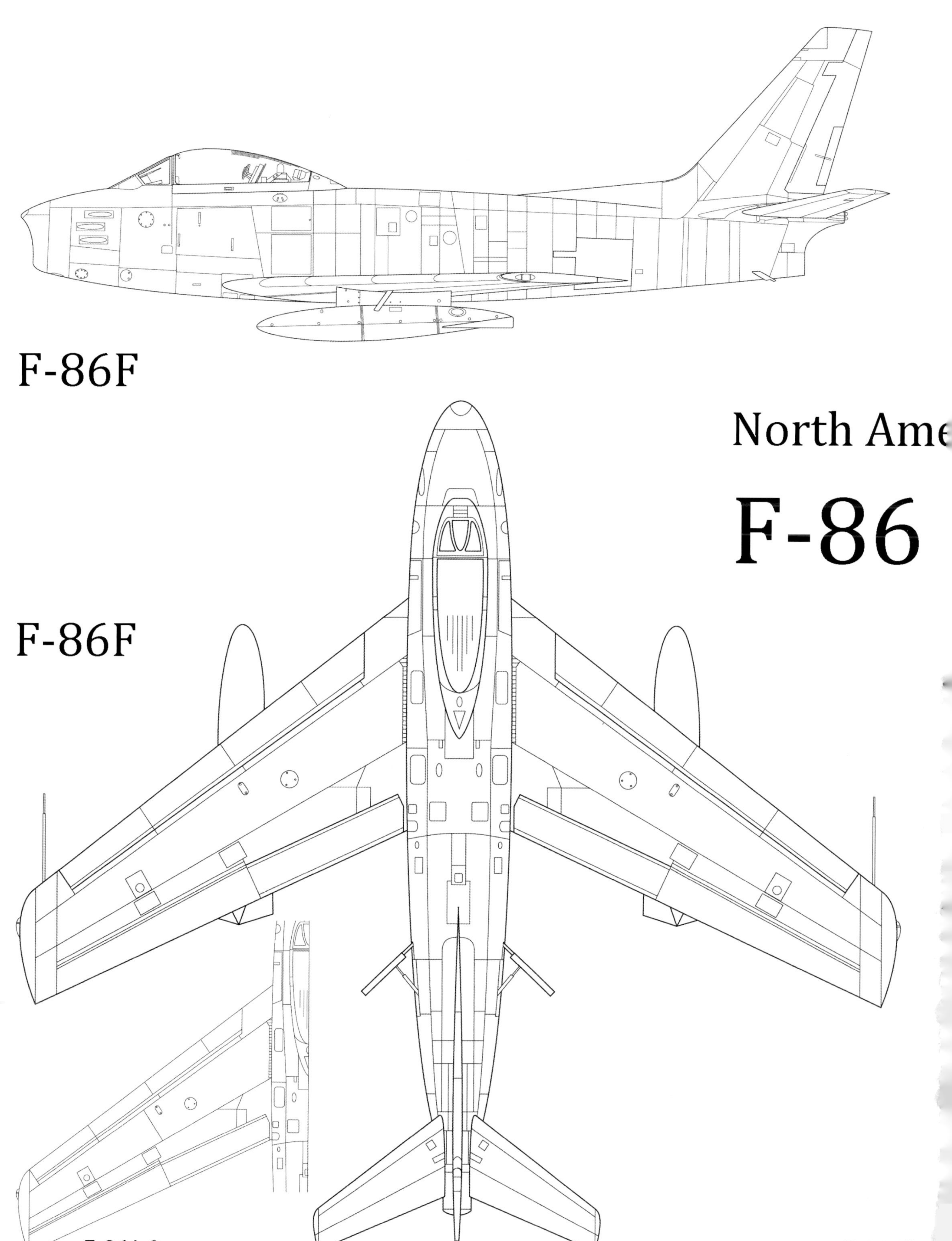
F-86F
North Ame
F-86
F-86F
F-86A &
Canadair Sabre MK.1-4
F-86F “6-
unslatted

THE CANADAIR F-86E SABRE 2

ONE 5,200 LB. S.T. GENERAL ELECTRIC J47

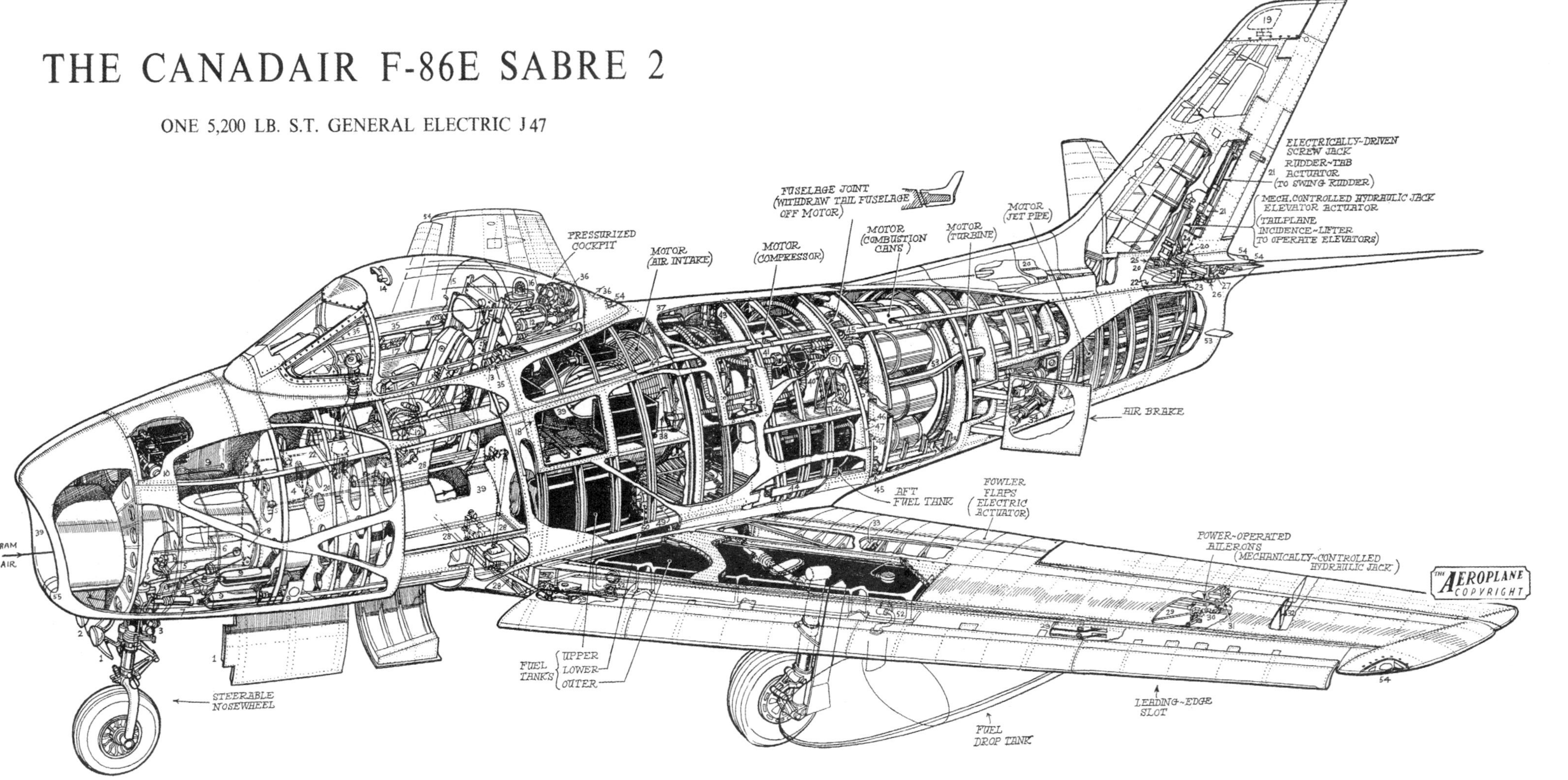

KEY

1. Nosewheel doors
2. Retracting lamps.
3. Hydraulic steering unit mechanical controller off rudder bars 4 via links and cables 5.
6. Main retraction jack.
7. Secondary retraction jack.
8. Wheel-well under air trunk.
9. Oxygen bottles (plus two on starboard side) and filler valve.
10. AC and DC system battery circuit-breakers and relay panel.
11. Armour and ejector seat with release.
12. Cartridge for ejector canopy and release.
13. Undercarriage warning horn
14. Hinged mirror.

Radio

15. Radio compass sense aerial.
16. Radio compass loop aerial.
17. Side panel.
18. Compartment contains IFF radio, radio-compass, aerial assembly, VHF radio-static converter.
19. Antenna (in fin)

Rudder Control

20. Cables from rudder pedals to rudder
21. Electrically-driven screw jack actuator to servo tab.

Elevator Control (Variable Incidence Tailplane Control)

22. Rod and cable connection from stick.
23. Bell crank to operate hydraulic supply valve 24.
24. Valve controls hydraulic jack to lift tailplane from spar 25.
26. Tailplane rear spar hinge.
27. Toggle gear automatically swings elevator with change of tailplane incidence.

Aileron Control

28. Rods from stick.
29. Cable control of hydraulic valve 30.
31. Operating jack regulated by valve 30.
32. Aileron air seal.

Flap Control

33. Electric actuator.

Air Brakes

34. Hydraulic operating jack electrically valved via restrictor, solenoid, control valve and accumulator, from cockpit handle.

Pressurized Cockpit

35. Canopy and windshield defrost.
36. Pressure regulator and exit.
37. Air mixing valve.
38. Cooling air bleed off air trunk 39.
40. Primary heat exchanger.
41. Motorized shut-off valve.
42. Trunnion mounting for engine.
43. Front suspension point.

Fuselage

44. Top and bottom longerons.
45. Four tail fuselage pin fixings.
46. Row of locating pegs between facing end frames 47 and 48.
49. Undercarriage wheel-well.
50. Underfloor vertical spine carrying undercarriage doors with fuel connecting pipe running through from front to aft fuel tanks (booster pump—transfer pump).
51. Fuel filler cap.
52. Fuel level transmitters
53. Fuel jettison.
54. Navigation lights.
55. Camera gun.

Drawing by
J. H. Clark, A.R.Ae.S.

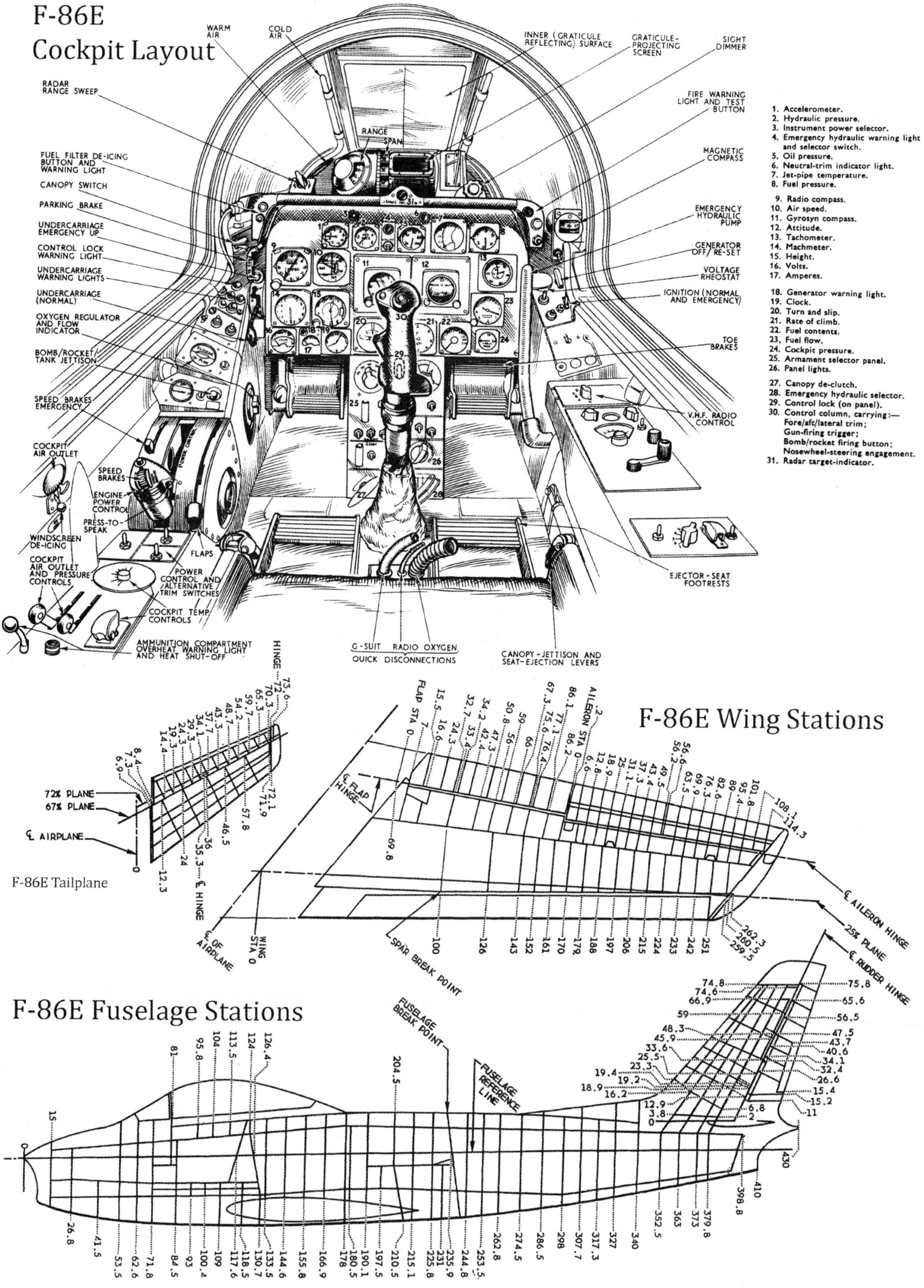
F-86E Cockpit Layout
WARM AIR
COLD AIR
INNER (GRATICULE REFLECTING) SURFACE
GRATICULE-PROJECTING SCREEN
SIGHT DIMMER
RADAR RANGE SWEEP
FIRE WARNING LIGHT AND TEST BUTTON
RANGE
SPAN
MAGNETIC COMPASS
FUEL FILTER DE-ICING BUTTON AND WARNING LIGHT
CANOPY SWITCH
PARKING BRAKE
EMERGENCY HYDRAULIC PUMP
UNDERCARRIAGE EMERGENCY UP
CONTROL LOCK WARNING LIGHT
GENERATOR OFF/RE-SET
UNDERCARRIAGE WARNING LIGHTS
VOLTAGE RHEOSTAT
UNDERCARRIAGE (NORMAL)
IGNITION (NORMAL AND EMERGENCY)
OXYGEN REGULATOR AND FLOW INDICATOR
TOE BRAKES
BOMB/ROCKET/TANK JETTISON
SPEED BRAKES EMERGENCY
V.H.F. RADIO CONTROL
COCKPIT AIR OUTLET
SPEED BRAKES
ENGINE POWER CONTROL
PRESS-TO-SPEAK
WINDSCREEN DE-ICING
FLAPS
COCKPIT AIR OUTLET AND PRESSURE CONTROLS
POWER CONTROL AND ALTERNATIVE TRIM SWITCHES
COCKPIT TEMP. CONTROLS
EJECTOR-SEAT FOOTRESTS
AMMUNITION COMPARTMENT OVERHEAT WARNING LIGHT AND HEAT SHUT-OFF
G-SUIT RADIO OXYGEN QUICK DISCONNECTIONS
CANOPY-JETTISON AND SEAT-EJECTION LEVERS
1. Accelerometer.
2. Hydraulic pressure.
3. Instrument power selector.
4. Emergency hydraulic warning light and selector switch.
5. Oil pressure.
6. Neutral-trim indicator light.
7. Jet-pipe temperature.
8. Fuel pressure.
9. Radio compass.
10. Air speed.
11. Gyrosyn compass.
12. Attitude.
13. Tachometer.
14. Machmeter.
15. Height.
16. Volts.
17. Amperes.
18. Generator warning light.
19. Clock.
20. Turn and slip.
21. Rate of climb.
22. Fuel contents.
23. Fuel flow.
24. Cockpit pressure.
25. Armament selector panel.
26. Panel lights.
27. Canopy de-clutch.
28. Emergency hydraulic selector.
29. Control lock (on panel).
30. Control column, carrying:— Fore/aft/lateral trim; Gun-firing trigger; Bomb/rocket firing button; Nosewheel-steering engagement.
31. Radar target-indicator.
F-86E Wing Stations
AILERON STA 0
FLAP STA 0
℄ FLAP HINGE
℄ AILERON HINGE
25% PLANE
℄ RUDDER HINGE
℄ OF AIRPLANE
WING STA 0
SPAR BREAK POINT
HINGE
72% PLANE
67% PLANE
℄ AIRPLANE
℄ HINGE
F-86E Tailplane
F-86E Fuselage Stations
FUSELAGE BREAK POINT
FUSELAGE REFERENCE LINE

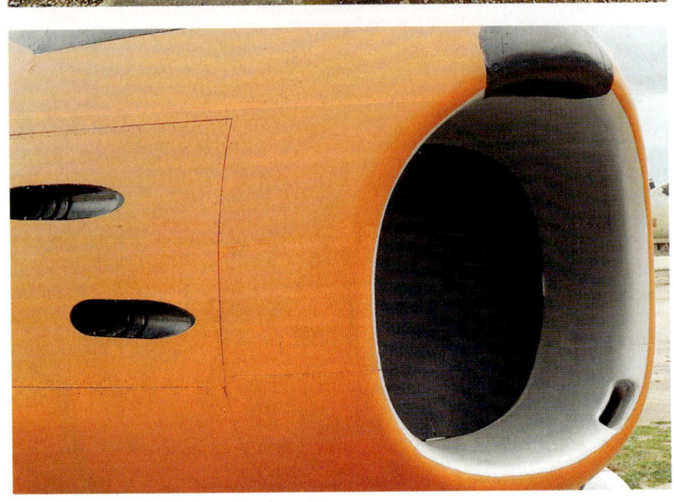

F-86H Sabre 53-1304 was manufactured by North American Aviation at the company's Columbus facility, and was delivered to the USAF on 8 April 1955. It is currently on static display at the March Field Air Museum at March AFB in California. *(Photos: Jeff Eddy)*

FORCE
CANOPY

U.S. AIR FORCE
WALKWAY

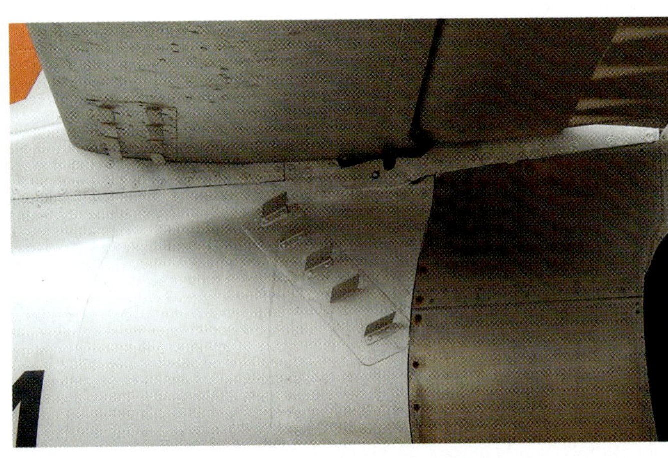

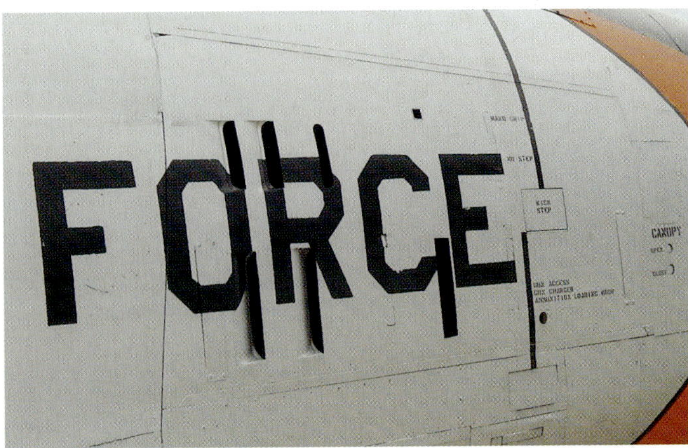

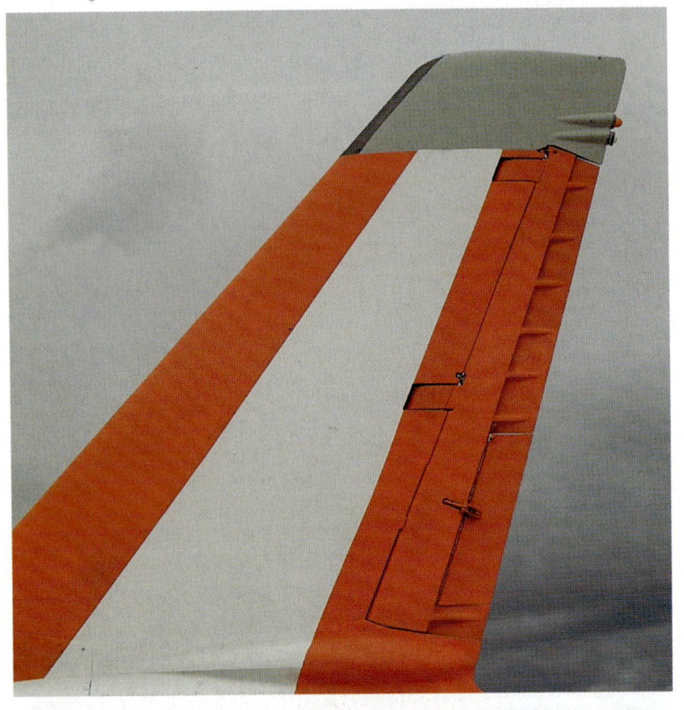

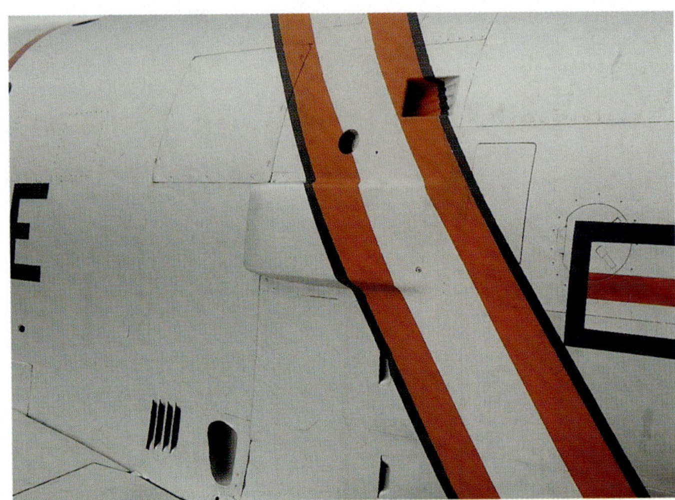

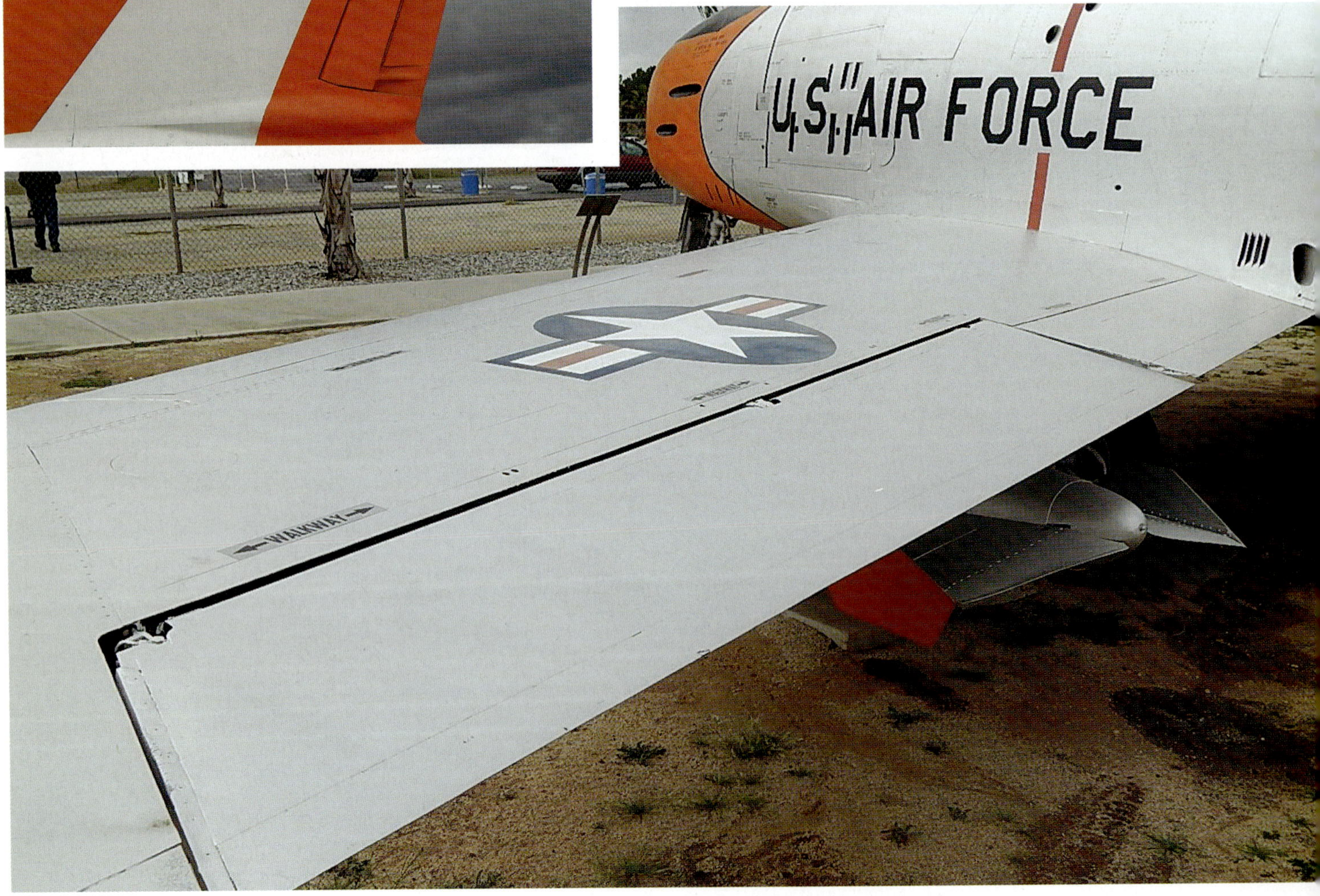

F-86H 53-1304 was first assigned to the 413th FDG at George AFB in 1955. It was transferred to Clovis AFB (312th FBW) in 1956 and then moved to Seymour Johnson AFB (83rd FDW) which was deployed to Eglin AFB. In 1957 it joined the Massachusetts ANG at Logan Airport before deploying to Phalsbourg AB in France during 1961 with the 102nd TFW. During 1963 it joined the Maryland ANG and after a spell with the 140th TFW at Cannon AFB, returned to the MD ANG (175th TFG) until June 1970 when it was removed from the USAF inventory.

(Photos: Jeff Eddy)

(Illustrations by Ted Williams – www.tedwilliamsaviationart.com)

▼ F-86A-5NA Sabre attached to the 336th Fighter Interceptor Squadron (FIS) USAF during Operation Stovepipe, Korea 1951.

▼ F-86A-5NA Sabre assigned to the 116th FIS, USAF stationed at RAF Bentwaters and RAF Shepherds Grove, England 1950

▼ RF-86A-5NA Sabre of the 15th Tactical Reconnaissance Squadron, USAF, K-14 Air Base in Korea 1952

▼ F-86D-35NA Sabre wearing the markings of the 339th FIS, USAF.

(Illustrations by Ted Williams – www.tedwilliamsaviationart.com)

▼ F-86E Sabre as flown by Capt. Pete Fernandez, the third highest-scoring ace in Korea, assigned to the 4th FIW, 334th FIS, USAF

▼ Canadair CL-13 Sabre F.Mk.4, No.122 Wing, RAF. Unique tail markings were reportedly applied to this aircraft, according to air and ground crews

▼ Canadair CL-13 Sabre Mk.6 assigned to Stab/JG 71 'Richthofen' Wittmundhafen, Germany, 1963

▼ F-86F Sabre assigned to the 310th FBS, USAF at Osan-ni Air Base, South Korea, 1958

Orenda 10 engine, adopted by Canadair for the Sabre

THE SERIES 10 ORENDA TURBOJET

6,355 LB. STATIC THRUST AT SEA LEVEL

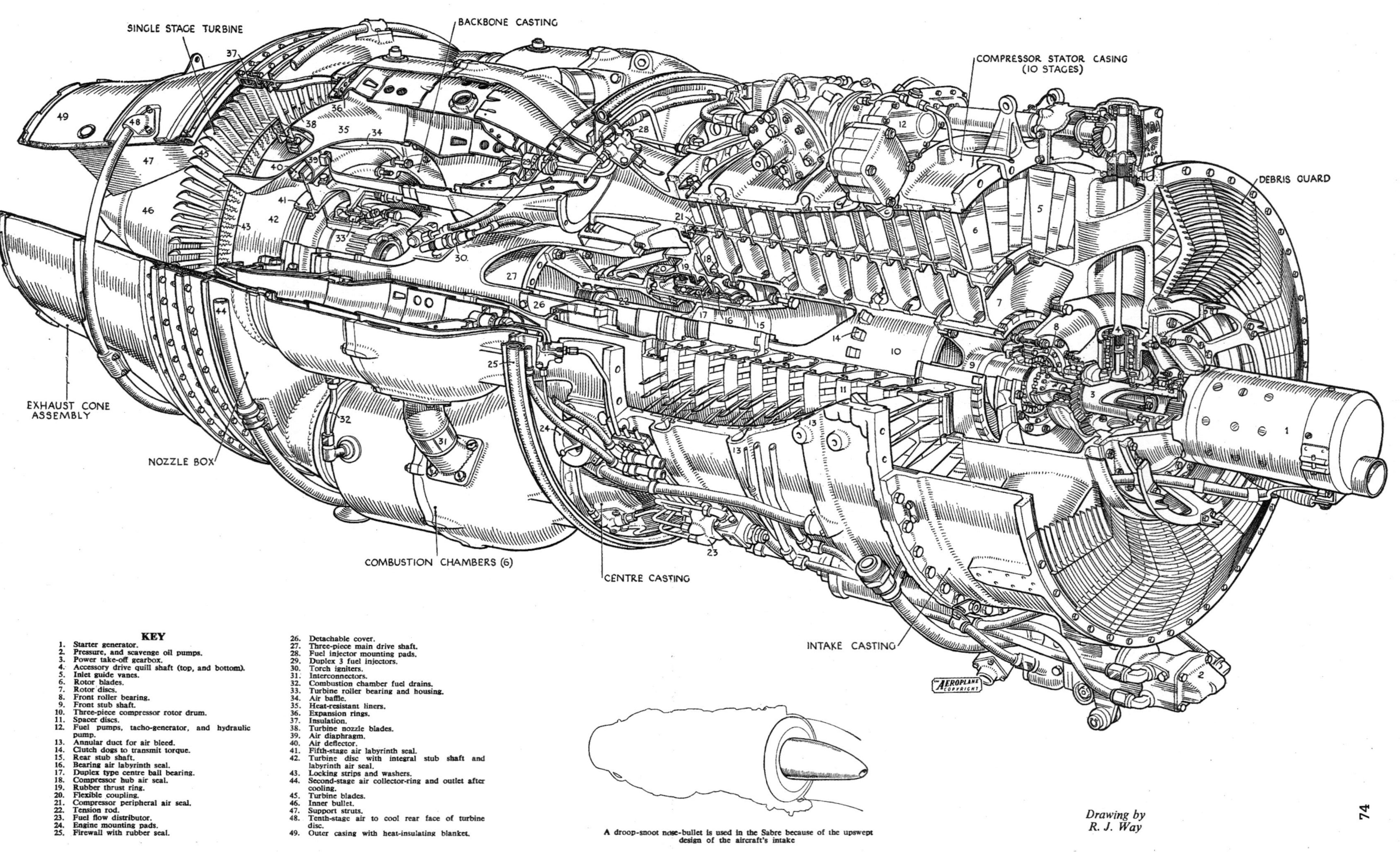

KEY

1. Starter generator.
2. Pressure, and scavenge oil pumps.
3. Power take-off gearbox.
4. Accessory drive quill shaft (top, and bottom).
5. Inlet guide vanes.
6. Rotor blades.
7. Rotor discs.
8. Front roller bearing.
9. Front stub shaft.
10. Three-piece compressor rotor drum.
11. Spacer discs.
12. Fuel pumps, tacho-generator, and hydraulic pump.
13. Annular duct for air bleed.
14. Clutch dogs to transmit torque.
15. Rear stub shaft.
16. Bearing air labyrinth seal.
17. Duplex type centre ball bearing.
18. Compressor hub air seal.
19. Rubber thrust ring.
20. Flexible coupling.
21. Compressor peripheral air seal.
22. Tension rod.
23. Fuel flow distributor.
24. Engine mounting pads.
25. Firewall with rubber seal.
26. Detachable cover.
27. Three-piece main drive shaft.
28. Fuel injector mounting pads.
29. Duplex 3 fuel injectors.
30. Torch igniters.
31. Interconnectors.
32. Combustion chamber fuel drains.
33. Turbine roller bearing and housing.
34. Air baffle.
35. Heat-resistant liners.
36. Expansion rings.
37. Insulation.
38. Turbine nozzle blades.
39. Air diaphragm.
40. Air deflector.
41. Fifth-stage air labyrinth seal.
42. Turbine disc with integral stub shaft and labyrinth air seal.
43. Locking strips and washers.
44. Second-stage air collector-ring and outlet after cooling.
45. Turbine blades.
46. Inner bullet.
47. Support struts.
48. Tenth-stage air to cool rear face of turbine disc.
49. Outer casing with heat-insulating blanket.

A droop-snoot nose-bullet is used in the Sabre because of the upswept design of the aircraft's intake

Drawing by R. J. Way

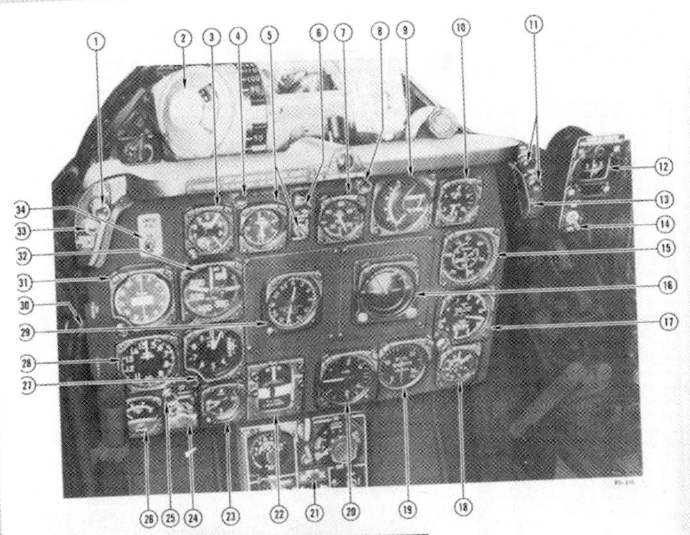

cockpit forward view

F-86E-1 THROUGH
F-86E-6 AIRPLANES

1. Fuel Filter Icing Warning Light
2. A-1CM Sight
3. Accelerometer
4. Instrument Power Warning Light*
5. Hydraulic Pressure Gage and Selector Switch
6. Alternate-on Warning Light (Flight Control Alternate Hydraulic System)
7. Oil Pressure Gage
8. Take-off (Trim) Position Indicator Light
9. Exhaust Temperature Gage
10. Fuel Pressure Gage*
11. Fire-warning Lights
12. Stand-by Compass
13. Fire-warning Light Test Button
14. Stand-by Compass Light Switch
15. Engine Tachometer
16. Attitude Indicator
17. Fuel Flowmeter
18. Cabin Pressure Altimeter*
19. Fuel Quantity Gage
20. Vertical Velocity Indicator (Rate-of-Climb)
21. Center Pedestal
22. Turn-and-Slip Indicator
23. Clock
24. Loadmeter
25. Generator Warning Light
26. Voltmeter
27. Altimeter
28. Machmeter
29. Directional Indicator (Slaved)
30. Landing Gear Emergency-up Button
31. Radio Compass
32. Airspeed Indicator
33. Fuel Filter Deicer Button
34. Emergency Fuel Switch*

*Some airplanes. (Refer to applicable text.)

F-86E-1-00-10

cockpit-left side

F-86E-1, F-86E-5, AND
F-86E-6 AIRPLANES

1. Circuit-breaker Panel
2. Ammunition Compartment Heat Emergency Shutoff Handle
3. Ammunition Compartment Overheat Warning Light
4. Console Floodlight
5. Side Air Outlet
6. Windshield Anti-icing Lever
7. Floodlight Control Rheostat
8. Rocket Intervalometer
9. Canopy Auxiliary Defrost Lever
10. Speed Brake Emergency Lever
11. Emergency Fuel Switch*
12. Instrument Panel Floodlight
13. Longitudinal Alternate Trim Switch
14. Left Forward Console
15. Parking Brake Handle
16. Canopy Switch
17. Landing Gear Emergency-up Button
18. Landing Gear Handle
19. Emergency Jettison Handle
20. Type D-2 Oxygen Regulator Panel
21. Throttle Friction Wheel
22. Wing Flap Lever
23. Throttle
24. Flight Control Switch
25. Rudder Trim Switch
26. Lateral Alternate Trim Switch
27. Cockpit Air Temperature Control Rheostat
28. Cabin Pressure Control Lever
29. Air Outlet Selector Lever
30. Cockpit Air Temperature Control Switch
31. Drop Tank Pressure Shutoff Valve
32. Anti-G Suit Pressure-regulating Valve

*Some airplanes. (Refer to applicable text.)

F-86E-1-00-2A

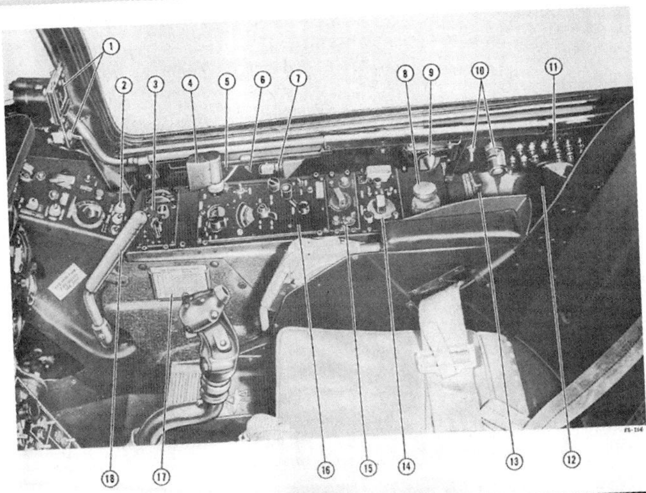

F-86E-1 THROUGH
F-86E-6 AIRPLANES

cockpit-right side

1. Stand-by Compass and Compass Light Switch
2. Right Forward Console
3. VHF Command Radio Control Panel*
4. Instrument Panel Floodlight
5. Side Air Outlet
6. Air Outlet Control Valve
7. Console Floodlight
8. Gun Sight Test Plug†
9. Instrument Ring Light Rheostat
10. Extension Light and Light Switch
11. Circuit-breaker Panel
12. Map Case
13. Densitometer Selector Valve
14. IFF Control Panel
15. UHF Command Radio Control Panel*
16. Radio Compass Control Panel
17. Radio Frequency Card
18. Emergency Hydraulic Hand-pump*

*Some airplanes. (Refer to applicable text.)
†F-86E-6 Airplanes

F-86E-1-00-15t

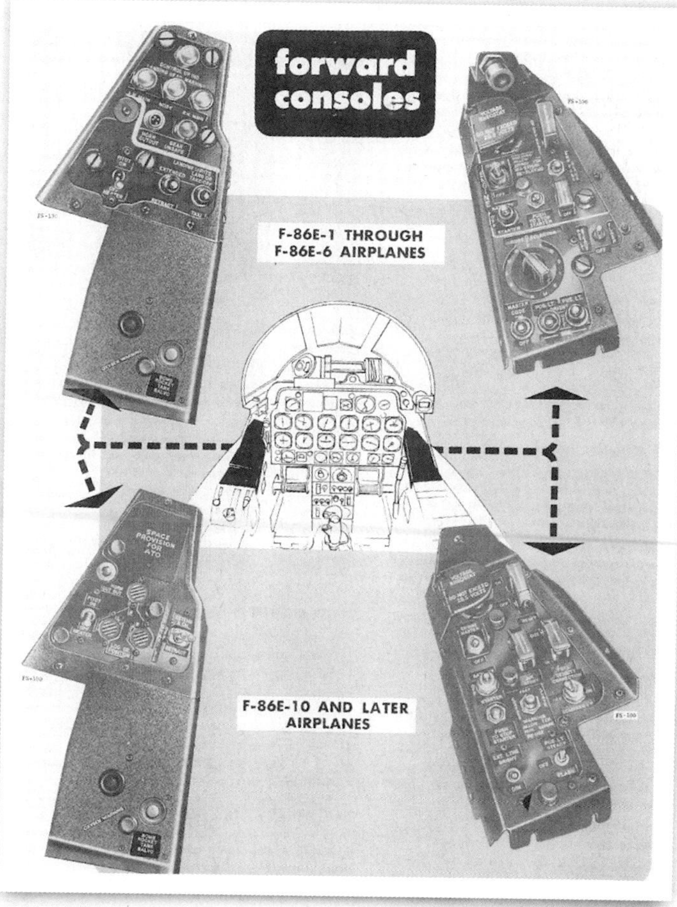

(Illustrations by Ted Williams – www.tedwilliamsaviationart.com)

▼ F-86F-10-NA Sabre as flown by the Minute Men aerobatic team, Colorado Air National Guard. The team received seven Sabres in 1958 and flew five aircraft at displays around the United States until July 1959

▼ RF-86F Sabre with the 67th Tactical Reconnaissance Wing, USAF, 1953. Yellow Korean theatre markings are outlined in black

▼ F-86F Sabre of the Japan Air Self Defense Force Blue Impulse aerobatic team

▼ F-86H-5-NA Sabre of the 1st FDS/413th FDW, USAF, located at George Air Force Base in California 1956.

(Illustrations by Ted Williams – www.tedwilliamsaviationart.com)

▼ F-86H-5-NA Sabre assigned to the 138th TFS, New York Air National Guard

▼ Fiat-manufactured F-86K Sabre assigned to ECTT 2/3 'Alpes', Armée de l'Air (French Air Force), 1963

▼ Fiat-manufactured F-86K Sabre wearing the markings of JG 74, Neuburg Air Base, Germany, 1963

▼ F-86L Sabre assigned to the Colorado Air National Guard

F-86L 50-0560 is part of a growing collection of airframes under the care of the March Field Air Museum, situated at March Air Force Base, Riverside, California. The aircraft has recently been repainted to carry markings representative of a typical USAF F-86D/L during the 1950s. *(Photos: Jeff Eddy)*

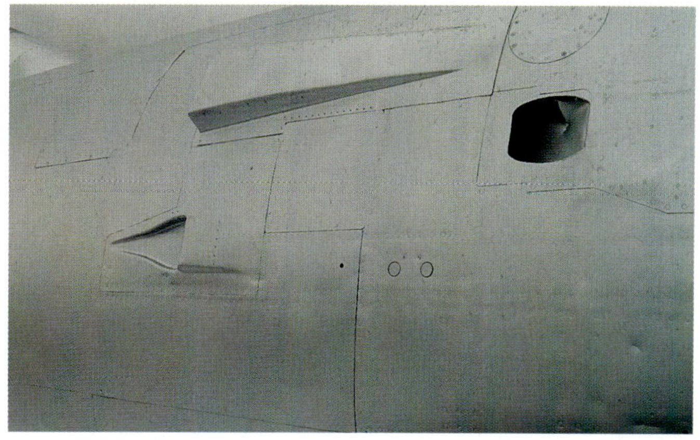

The March Field Museum's F-86L serial number 50-0560 was delivered to the Air Force 3555th Fighter Training Wing during December 1952 as an F-86D model. Undergoing conversion in 1957, it was assigned to the re-designated 3555th Combat Crew Training Wing. Three years later, 50-0560 was transferred to Norton AFB, California and retired. Used as a static display at Oro Grande Park the aircraft was salvaged and restored by the March Field Air Museum in 1996. F-86L 50-0560 is currently displayed in the livery of the 3555th Combat Crew Training Wing, its first assignment as an F-86L model. *(Photos: Jeff Eddy)*

(Illustrations by Ted Williams – www.tedwilliamsaviationart.com)

▼ F-86L Sabre assigned to the 496th FIS, 86th FBW, USAF

▼ FJ-1 Fury assigned to Fighter Squadron VF-5A, United States Navy, aboard the USS *Boxer* (CVA-21) during 1948.

▼ FJ-1 Fury assigned to Naval Air Reserve Wing NARW-88, US Navy, based at NAS Olathe in Kansas, 1953

▼ FJ-2B Fury wearing the markings of the Naval Air Test Center, based at NAS Patuxent River, Maryland, 1953

(Illustrations by Ted Williams – www.tedwilliamsaviationart.com)

▼ FJ-3 Fury assigned to the US Navy Guided Missile Group GMGRU-1 during 1956

▼ FJ-4 Fury allocated to Utility Squadron VU-7 'Redtails' based at NAS Brown Field in 1960

▼ FJ-4 Fury assigned to VMF-334, United States Marine Corps, based at MCAS Cherry Point

▼ F-4B Fury assigned to VA-126, United States Navy, based at NAS Miramar during 1958

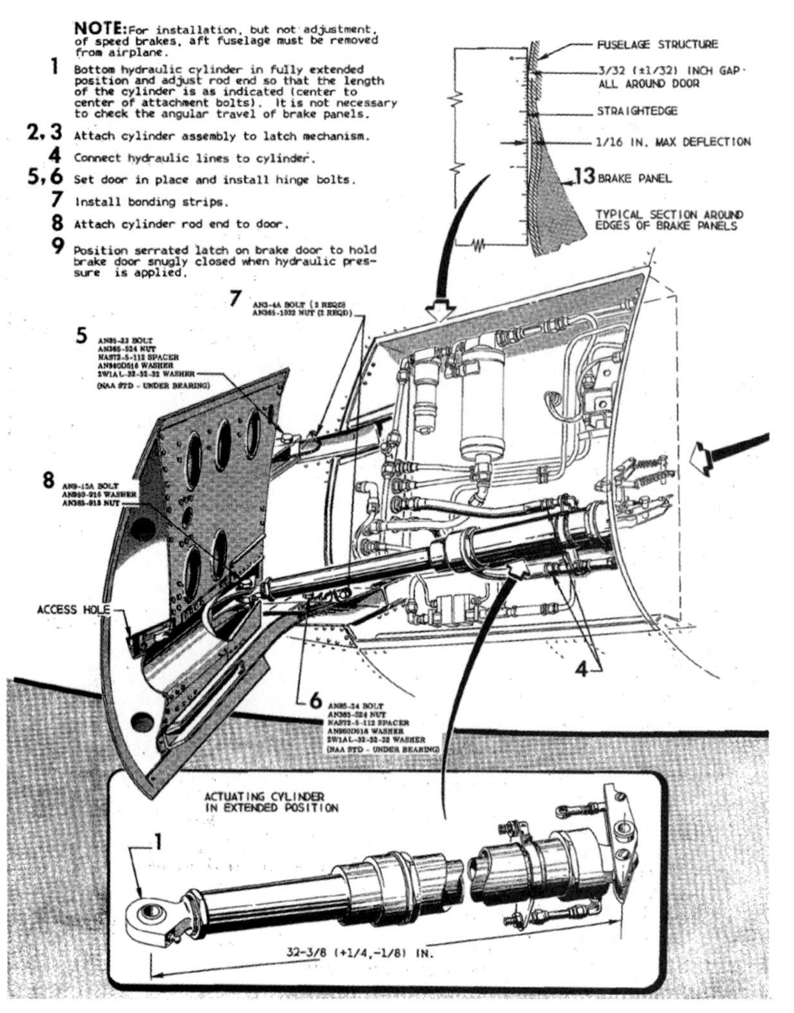

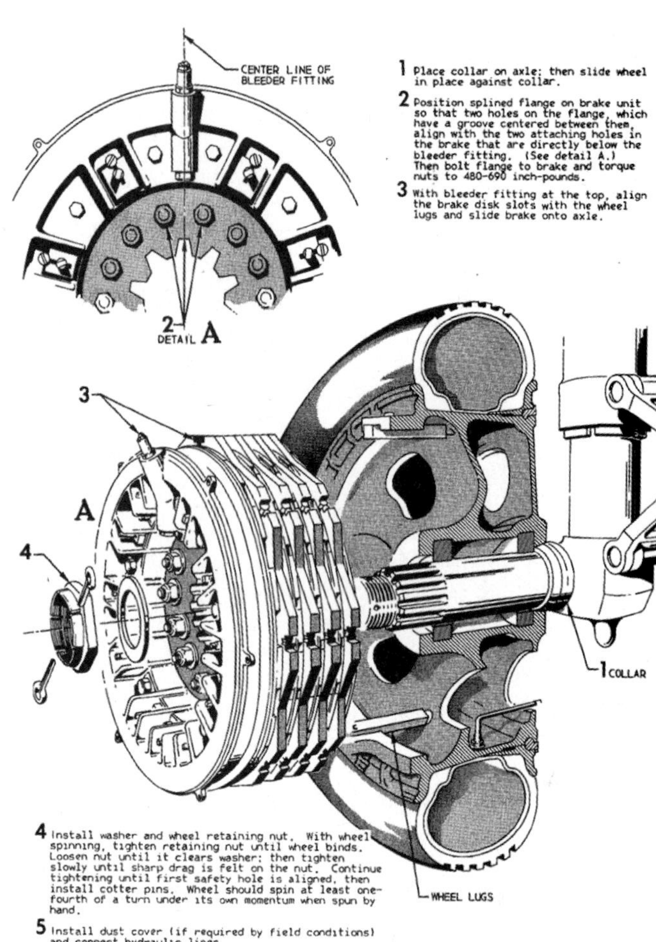

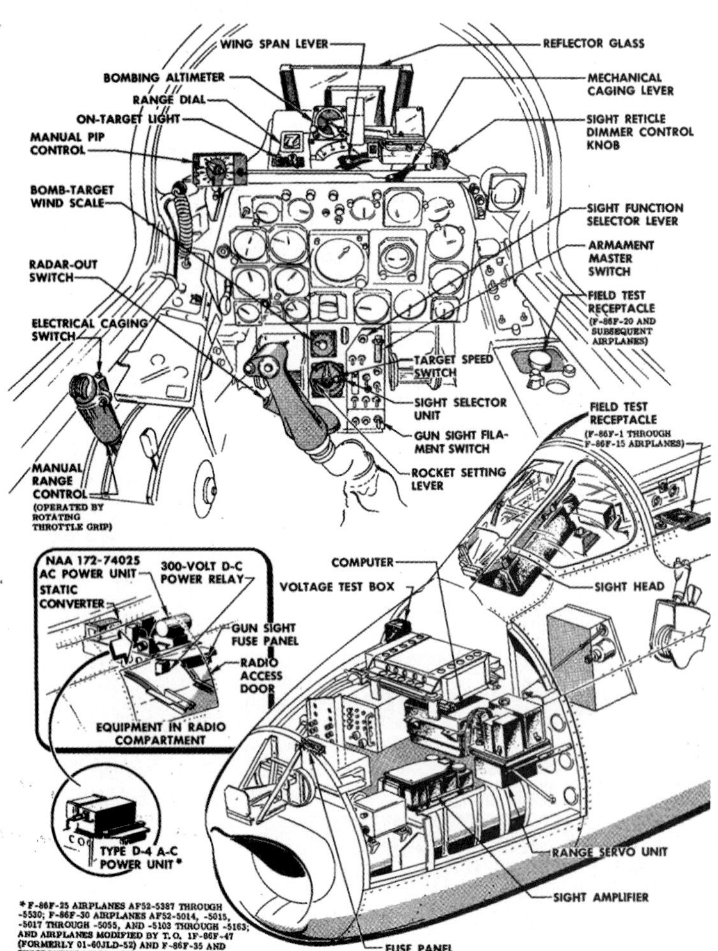

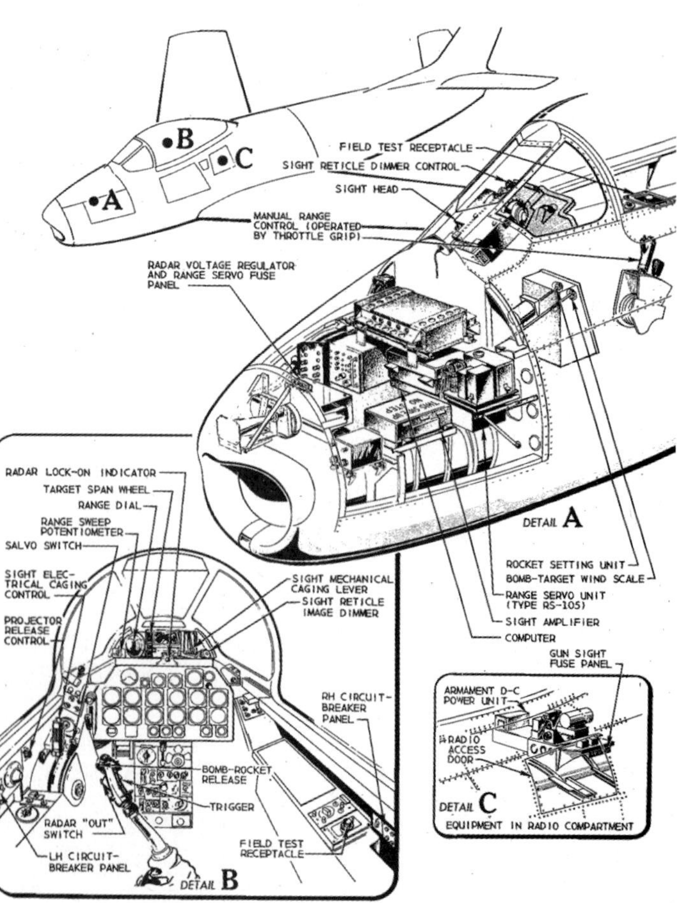

Extracts from the F-86 Sabre technical manuals, produced for the USAF by NAA

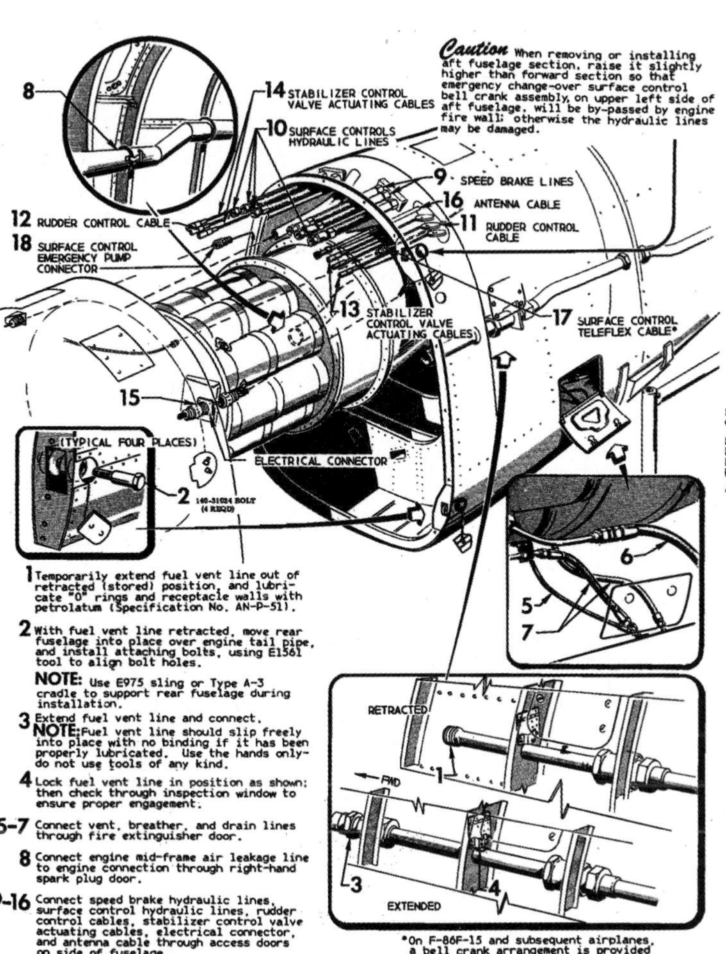

RADAR "OUT" SWITCH
RADAR "ON TARGET" INDICATOR*
RANGE SWEEP CONTROL
VOLTAGE TEST BOX
TRANSMITTER
WAVE GUIDE QUICK-DISCONNECT
RANGE POWER UNIT
RADAR POWER CIRCUIT BREAKER
RADAR VOLTAGE REGULATOR AND RANGE SERVO FUSE PANEL
ANTENNA
VOLTAGE REGULATOR

NOTE: The subdued units shown are components of the A-1CM gun sight which are associated with the AN/APG-30 radar set.

*On F-86F-15 and subsequent airplanes, the "ON TARGET" indicator is installed in the A-4 sighthead.

EXPENDABLE RUBBER PLUG (TYPICAL)
TORQUE NUT TO 90 INCH-POUNDS.
BLAST TUBE CLAMP
RIGHT GUN COMPARTMENT
LEFT BLAST PANEL
EXPENDED LINK CHUTES
FLEXIBLE AMMUNITION FEED CHUTES
EXPENDED CASE AND LINK COMPARTMENT
AMMUNITION CONTAINER COMPARTMENT
EXPENDED CASE AND LINK COMPARTMENT
A
RIGHT BLAST PANEL
AIR LINE FOR RIGHT SIDE GUN CHARGERS
MOUNTING STRAPS
AIR BOTTLE
WING NUTS
AIR LINE FOR LEFT SIDE GUN CHARGERS
COMPRESSOR
PRESSURE REGULATOR VALVE
AIR FILLER VALVE
MOISTURE DRAIN
RELIEF VALVE
OIL SUMP CUP SCREW (FINGER TIGHTEN ONLY)
AIR LINE TO RH GUNS
AIR LINE TO LH GUNS
PRESSURE REGULATOR VALVE
AIR LINE TO BOTTLE OUTPUT
PRESSURE GAGE
FILLER VALVE
AIR LINE TO BOTTLE INPUT

DETAIL A AIR COMPRESSOR AND AIR BOTTLE

PNEUMATIC GUN CHARGERS AND RELATED EQUIPMENT INSTALLED ON THE FOLLOWING AIRPLANES ONLY: F-86F-1 THRU F-86F-20 AIRPLANES, F-86F-25 AIRPLANES AF51-13170 THRU -13510 AND AF52-5272 THRU -5277, -5279 THRU -5290, -5292, -5294, -5295, -5297, -5298, -5300 THRU -5302, AND -5304; AND F-86F-30 AIRPLANES AF52-4305 THRU -4963.

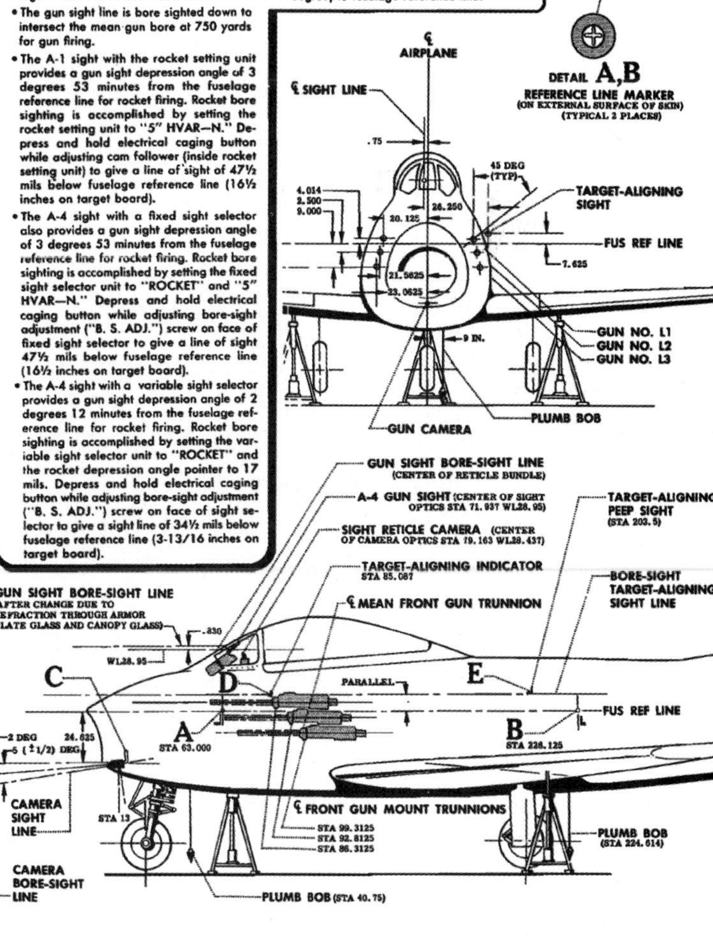

GLOBAL ACCLAIM

The F-86 Sabre's success is exported around the world

Royal Canadian Air Force Canadair Sabre Mk.4s in post-delivery unpainted finish. *(Photo: Key Collection)*

F-86Es of the Fuerza Aérea Argentina *(Photo: Tim McLelland collection)*

The F-86 Sabre's importance to the United States Air Force and Navy is matched by its influence overseas. The Sabre was exported to many countries, and built under license in very significant numbers. Most notably, it played a major part in the Military Assistance Program (MAP) or Mutual Defense Assistance Program (MDAP) in which the United States supplied aircraft to countries on a lease basis in order to improve political stability across the globe, but particularly in Europe, where the Cold War with the Soviets was developing. The full story of the Sabre's export success cannot be described only within the terms of MDAP, as many other airframes were also exported, often as refurbished aircraft that had previously served with the USAF.

Argentina

Some 28 surplus F-86F-30s were delivered to the Fuerza Aérea Argentina (FAA) in 1960, the first of these being received on 26 September 1960. The fleet wore serial numbers C-101 to C-128. FAA Sabres saw action in helping to suppress a 1962 coup attempt against the established government, attacking the naval base at Punta Indio and destroying a Navy C-54 on the ground, helping to end the coup. Argentina attempted to sell F-86Fs to Venezuela in 1976, but the deal was embargoed by the United States, the Sabres then being offered to Uruguay, although the plan was abandoned just before they were due to be delivered. In 1982 when Argentina invaded the Falklands, deployment of A-4 Skyhawks resulted in ten Sabres being kept airworthy for local air defence duties in Argentina, but following a crash in June 1986 (C-120 suffering a wing structure failure), the fleet was withdrawn. Some of these former FAA aircraft have now been restored in civilian hands and continue to fly in the USA.

Australia

Although Australia was keen to acquire the British Hawker P.1081, this plan was abandoned in October 1950, and purchase of the Sabre was approved on 22 February 1951. During October 1951, an order for 72 aircraft was placed with the Commonwealth Aircraft

Royal Australian Air Force Sabre Mk.31s, assigned to No 3 Squadron, RAAF Williamstown *(Photo: Key Collection)*

Bolivian Air Force F-86F, formerly with the Venezuelan Air Force. ***(Photo: Tim McLelland collection)***

Corporation and 100 sets of major components were ordered from NAA for licence production in Australia. Significant design changes were needed in order to adapt the Sabre to Australian requirements, including additional engine power and larger-calibre armament. The General Electric J47-GE-27 engine was replaced by a Rolls-Royce Avon R.A.7, rated at 7,500lb thrust, requiring the air intake to be increased in size, and resulting in the lowering and re-contouring of the forward fuselage. The new (lighter) engine had to be positioned further aft in order to maintain centre of gravity, resulting in a slightly longer forward fuselage and a shortened rear fuselage, redesigned to support the engine jet pipe so that neither tail plane inertia loads or tail unit flight loads would be transferred to the engine. The much greater thrust of the Avon also required a larger exhaust nozzle, and this increased the depth of the rear fuselage slightly. However the overall length of the CAC Sabre remained identical to that of the F-86F. In August 1952 a decision was made to adopt a pair of 30mm ADEN cannon as primary armament, and this required some further structural redesign of the fuselage. The cannon were mounted in the original 0.50in machine gun bays, but staggered, with the starboard weapon mounted inverted and some eight inches forward of the port weapon. The forward fuselage had to be strengthened considerably to withstand the heavier amount of recoil from the high-velocity cannon. The wing design was a standard F-86E/F component with leading-edge slats, and the elevator was a standard all-flying tail as employed on the F-86E/F. The first prototype Australian Sabre (CA-26 A94-101) was designated CA-26 and flew for the first time on 3 August 1953, and some 22 Sabre Mk.30s (A94-901 to A94-922) were produced. The next production version was the CA-27 Mk.31, fitted with a '6-3' wing, some 21 Sabre Mk.31s being built (A94-922 to A94-942). The last 28 aircraft on the original RAAF order were completed as Mk.32s (A94-943 to A94-970) featuring Australian-built Avon 26 engines, rated at 7,500lb combined with '6-3' wings and an additional pair of wing pylons. An additional 20 Mk.32s (A94-971 to A94-990) were ordered in July 1957, and a final order for 21 Mk.32s (A94-351 to A94-371) was issued in 1959. The last RAAF Sabre was retired in July 1971 and 18 Sabre Mk.32s were supplied to the Royal Malaysian Air Force. The first Sabres arrived in Malaysia in October 1969. No 11 Squadron flew the type until April 1978, when they were finally retired. Five were transferred to

RCAF Sabre F.Mk.2s from No.441 Squadron, RAF North Luffenham in 1952.
(Photo: Key Collection)

Camouflaged Sabres from No.622 Squadron RCAF. based in France during 1957. *(Photo: Key Collection)*

Colombian Air Force Canadair Sabre Mk.6. *(Photo: Tim McLelland collection)*

Indonesia in August 1976, and A94-983 was returned to Australia for restoration to flying condition for the RAAF Historic Flight. During February 1973, the Indonesian government ordered 18 former RAAF Sabres for the Indonesian Republican Air Force. A further five aircraft were purchased from Malaysia in July 1976 as attrition replacements and these remained in use until the early 1980s.

Bolivia

A batch of nine former Venezuelan AF F-86Fs was transferred to Bolivia in October 1973, receiving serials 650 to 658. Thanks to a combination of accidents and spares shortages, only four remained in use by 1987 and hopes of acquiring Argentina's Sabres were thwarted because of the Falklands War and subsequent fatigue problems. The remaining three aircraft soldiered on into the late 1980s after which they were purchased by Texas Air Command in the USA for restoration and resale on the civilian market.

Canada

The Sabre was an obvious choice for the Royal Canadian Air Force, but with some political pressure to avoid purchasing an American machine (a British purchase being preferred), the Canadian government proposed licence-production of the Sabre in Canada. This was an arrangement that suited the US, as NAA was already struggling to maintain production capacity. During August 1949, the Canadian government ordered 100 examples of the Sabre from Canadair. Under the provisions of the agreement, the Sabres were to be assembled at the Canadair plant at Cartierville from drawings and components supplied by North American. The Canadian-built aircraft were to be almost identical to the F-86A with a 5,200lb General Electric J47-GE-13 engine. The first Sabres assembled at Cartierville were designated as the CL-13 Sabre Mk.1. With RCAF serial 19101, it made its maiden flight on 9 August 1950.

RCAF Golden Hawks aerobatic team Sabres, in gold finish with red trim. *(Photo: Tim McLelland collection)*

Royal Danish Air Force F-86Ds. *(Photos: Tim McLelland collection)*

Only one Sabre Mk.1 was built, and the first Sabre version to be built in quantity was the CL-13 Sabre Mk.2, the equivalent of an F-86E-1. A total of 350 Mk.2s was built between January 1951 and August 1952 (19102 to 19199 and 19201 to 19452). RCAF Sabre operations began with No. 410 Squadron at Dorval, where the first aircraft arrived in April 1951. Nos. 411 and 413 Squadrons followed in the summer of 1951. When the USAF suffered a shortage of Sabres during the Korean War, and in February 1952, the USAF purchased 60 Sabre Mk.2s from Canada, designated as the F-86E-6-CAN. North American Aviation initiated company project NA-167 in August 1949, exploring the installation of an Orenda engine in F-86A-5-NA 49-1069 (sometimes referred to as the F-86J). Tests were encouraging, and the 100th Sabre Mk.2 (19200) was modified to accommodate a 6,000lb Orenda 3 engine, requiring some changes to the fuselage structure in order to increase intake airflow. This modified aircraft was re-designated as the Canadair Sabre Mk 3. The Orenda engine was to be introduced in the Sabre Mk.4 production variant version but delays in engine development resulted in retention of the F-86E airframe and the J47-GE-13 engine for the Mk.4. Consequently, the Sabre Mk.4 was largely similar to the Mk.2, with only a few minor modifications. Some 438 Mk.4s were built (19453 to 19890) and many of these aircraft (plus some Mk.2 airframes) were retrofitted with the '6-3' wing. The first production Sabre to employ the Orenda engine was the CL-13A Mk.5 variant, which was powered by the 6,355lb Orenda 10. Fitted with a '6-3' wing and a pair of tiny wing fences, it was an aerodynamic equivalent of the F-86F-30. The first Sabre Mk.5 (23001) made its maiden flight on 30 July 1953. A total of 370 Mk.5s was built, serials 23001 to 23370. The final production version was the CL-13B Sabre Mk.6 with a two-stage Orenda 14 delivering 7,275lb thrust. Slightly lighter than the Mk.5, the Mk.6 became the best performer of the Canadair Sabre family, with a top speed of 710mph and a service ceiling of 55,000 feet, some 7,000 feet greater than that of the F-86F. 292 Mk.6s were initially built for the RCAF (23371 to 23662) and 90 additional Mk.6s were later procured for the RCAF (23663 to 23752). The Sabre Mk.6 remained in regular service with the RCAF until 1963 with the last example being retired on 9 December 1968. Subsequent Sabre Mk.6 production was for export, the final aircraft being completed on 9 October 1958.

Colombia

With the US government reluctant to fuel an arms race in the region, it was Canadair that agreed to supply Colombia with six Sabre Mk.6s, and these were completed in May 1956. They were joined by three F-86s in 1963, these being former Spanish Air Force machines that had been returned to the US, fitted with less powerful J47 engines that shared no commonality with the FAC's other Sabres. Accidents and spares shortages soon began to have an effect on operations and in 1966 the surviving examples were retired, their fighter role lying dormant until Mirages were acquired in 1972.

Denmark

Having formed an independent air force on 27 May 1950, Denmark received 38 former USAF F-86D-30 and F-86D-35 aircraft as part of an MDAP agreement, in 1958. Conversion onto the type began in June of that year with Eskadril 723 at Aalborg. The unit's aircraft received codes ABA to AB-T while the second unit to re-equip (Eskadril 726) were given codes AL-A to AL-T. A further 21 F-86Ds were delivered in May 1960 for Eskadril 728 (coded in the SI range) and although the aircraft remained mostly unchanged from their previous service with the USAF, they received Martin-Baker ejection seats and launch rails for AIM-9 Sidewinder AAMs. Three F-86Ds

F-86K Sabre, Armée de l'Air *(Photo: Tim McLelland collection)*

were acquired from France's Châteauroux storage facility in March 1962 to act as spares sources for the active fleet, and operations continued until March 1966 when the last Danish unit to operate the Sabre (Eskadril 728) retired its aircraft.

Ethiopia

Three F-86Fs were delivered to the IEAF (Imperial Ethiopian Air Force) during July 1960, followed by six more in September, all having come from former USAF stocks via Spain. By December 1960 these Sabres were engaged in combat, attacking rebel positions in Addis Ababa, and less than a year later the aircraft were again assigned to combat operations, with four aircraft being sent to the Congo as part of a US peacekeeping effort. Despite spares shortages, Ethiopia offered to assign more Sabres to the Congo in 1962 but by the end of that year their fighter cover duties were taken over by Iranian aircraft. The Sabres saw further action in 1964 during the Horn of Africa war and efforts were made to acquire further aircraft. However the US became reluctant to supply them and eventually a batch of up to 22 F-86Fs was supplied by Iran. These were brought into service to augment the existing fleet, resulting in the Sabre remaining active until 1977, although some reports suggest that a few may have been used during the war with Somalia, which continued into 1978.

France

Although the French Air Force anticipated delivery of indigenously manufactured aircraft (the Vautour and Mirage), delays in development and production prompted a decision to acquire the F-86K Sabre as an interim fighter. The F-86K was a direct development of the USAF's F-86D, designed for

export. Partly because of a reluctance to export the aircraft's A-4 Fire Control System and partly because it was likely to be a troublesome system for 'customer' countries to operate, a less sophisticated version of the F-86D was proposed, with a new MG-4 Fire Control System linked to four 20mm cannon, in place of the aircraft's usual rocket projectile pack. The first of 60 F-86Ks (all built with US components by Fiat in Italy) arrived in September 1956, with deliveries being completed by the following June. After settling into service, the F-86K fleet was overhauled and modified at Fiat's Turin plant in 1959, with wing tip and leading edge extensions being fitted. Unusually, most of the F-86K fleet was also repainted at this stage to feature a bright red and white band across the fuselage sides, intended to provide better conspicuity, the French Air Force having concluded that European weather conditions created a significant collision danger. Further modifications were made by Fiat in 1960 to equip the F-86Ks with Sidewinder missiles although only part of the fleet was upgraded to this standard. The Sabres remained active until 1962 when the last examples were retired in October, and returned to USAF control, although most airframes remained in France in storage. Those that were not subsequently transferred elsewhere were destroyed as part of MDAP arrangements and just one example now remains in France, on display at the Musée de l'Air in Paris.

West Germany

Following agreement to form a new German air force in October 1954, the F-86K was selected for the Luftwaffe's all-weather interception role and the F-86F for the day fighter role. Training in Germany began with USAF F-86Fs during 1955 although the first German Sabre didn't arrive until 1957, when

Luftwaffe F-86 Sabre Mk.5 and Mk.6. and F-86K all-weather interceptor. *(Photos: Tim McLelland collection)*

the first of 75 Canadian-built Sabre Mk.5 aircraft was delivered, via overhaul at Renfrew in Scotland. The first Sabre Mk.6 was delivered in September 1958 and as the Luftwaffe's day fighter units slowly worked up to operational level, a fleet of 88 F-86Ks had also been delivered, although only 57 aircraft actually entered service. The Sabre Mk.5 and Mk.6 remained in use with the Luftwaffe for some time but the F-86K enjoyed only a brief period of service, as the air arm was soon preparing to receive the first examples of the F-104G Starfighter. The last F-86K was withdrawn by JG 74 on 5 January 1966 and most of the surviving airframes were eventually transferred to Venezuela. Some Sabre Mk.6s were modified to carry Martin-Baker Mk.5 ejection seat (requiring a re-shaped canopy) while others were equipped to carry the AIM-9 Sidewinder missile. Operational use continued until December 1966 at which stage the last remaining aircraft were withdrawn, to be replaced by Fiat G91s. However a small number of Sabres continued to fly with a Condor, a civilian contractor, tasked with the provision of aerial target facilities. Seven aircraft were converted into target tugs and these remained active in support of Luftwaffe fighter units until April 1974.

Greece

The Elliniki Polemiki Aeroporia (Hellenic Air Force) was supplied with a fleet of 104 F-86E(M) aircraft, these being overhauled Canadair Sabre Mk.2s, the first of which arrived at Elefsina Air Base on 2 July 1954. Replacing the F-84 Thunderjet, they first equipped 341 Mira (squadron), followed by 342 and 343 Miras, after which all of the Sabre units moved to Tanagra. Unlike its neighbours in Turkey (who were offered F-86Es and F-100 Super Sabres) Greece was offered an additional fleet of 35 F-86Ds, and the first of these arrived at Elefsina on 17 May 1960, where it joined 337 Mira. In 1961 343 Mira exchanged its F-86E aircraft for the F-86D. Both Sabre variants remained in use for a relatively short amount of time, the last of the F-86Es being replaced by F-5s in January 1966, while the final F-86D was withdrawn in May 1967, although many of these aircraft (including some F-86Es) were retained until the 1990s as ground decoys on various Hellenic Air Force airfields.

Honduras

Following the 1969 'Soccer War' Honduras made great efforts to improve its air force, starting with the purchase of Ouragans from El Salvador. Honduras negotiated the sale of some Super Mystères from Israel but the deal took time to finalise so a fleet of eight former Yugoslav Canadair CL-13 MK.4s was obtained (plus two F-86Fs for use as spares), as a suitable alternative. Despite the Israeli deal eventually going ahead, the Sabre purchase was completed. The Fuerza Aérea Hondureña also received five former Venezuelan F-86Ks in 1969, but only four were made airworthy, and with the Super Mystères having arrived from Israel, the Sabres were used as fighter-bombers until the 1980s, thanks to technical support from Venezuela, which kept the dwindling fleet airworthy. However, it is likely

Hellenic Air Force (Elliniki Polemiki Aeroporia) F-86E and F-86D Sabres. *(Photos: Tim McLelland collection)*

that the more complex F-86Ks were withdrawn much sooner.

Indonesia

Australia transferred 18 former RAAF Sabre Mk.32s to Indonesia in 1972, and provided technical support as part of the arrangement, resulting in the first aircraft being delivered during February 1973. As part of the Angkatan Udara Republik Indonesia (AURI) they were given serials F-86-01 to F-86-18 and all were assigned to No.14 Squadron at Iswahyudi Air Base. Three years later a further five Sabres were acquired from the Royal Malaysian Air Force, and the type remained in service until 1980 when the surviving examples (some having been lost in flying accidents) were retired and assigned to ground training duties, having been replaced by deliveries of F-5s.

Iran

A fleet of 52 F-86F-25 Sabres was supplied to the Imperial Iranian Air Force (IIAF) as part of a MAP agreement made in 1960. Most of the aircraft were delivered from Fiat's Turin plant, where they had been refurbished after having been in temporary storage at Châteauroux in France, following withdrawal from USAF service there in 1956. Allocated serials 3-100 to 3-151, the Sabres replaced Thunderjets with the 1st Tactical Fighter Squadron at Mehrabad and the 3rd TFS at Vahdati Air Base. The 2nd FTS and 4th TFS also re-equipped and conversion to the Sabre was completed in the summer of 1961. Further Sabres were to have been supplied but this plan was abandoned in favour of the F-5 'Freedom Fighter'. Four IIAF Sabres participated in UN operations in the Congo during 1963, and in 1966 Israel Aircraft Industries was awarded a contract to

Sabre A94-361 being prepared for Indonesia as F-8601 *(Photo: Dave Masterson)*

overhaul part of the IIAF Sabre fleet at Lod Airport in Israel. A second similar contract was agreed later that year. Unusually, Iran announced the acquisition of 90 former Luftwaffe Sabres in February 1966, but this story was eventually revealed to be part of an arrangement for the supply of these aircraft to Pakistan. The IIAF Sabre fleet gradually contracted as more F-5s came into service, and the final operational use of the F-86F took place in 1971.

Italy

Some 180 former RAF Sabres were shipped to Italy, beginning in 1955. Upgraded to F-86E(M) standard, one slatted-wing Mk,2 was also delivered. The first Aeronautica Militare (AM) unit to transition to the F-86E(M) was the 4th Aerobrigata, based at Pratica di Mare. In 1961, the Frecce Tricolori (Tricolor Arrows) aerobatic team was formed with six F-86E(M)s. Five Italian Sabres were dispatched to the Belgian Congo in 1963 to support UN peacekeeping operations there, and a detachment of Philippine Air Force personnel operated these AM Sabres from February to June 1963.

The last F-86E(M) left AM service in March 1965. Italy also received two YF-86Ks and 63 Fiat-assembled F-86Ks during 1956-57. The first two operational aircraft (MM6192 and MM6193) were delivered from Turin on 2 November 1955 and the final AI F-86K was delivered by Fiat in October 1957. Twenty-two former French F-86Ks were assigned to Italy in 1962, followed by eight former Royal Netherlands Air Force machines in 1963. Retirement of the F-86K began during 1964, when Italian Air Force units began to

Imperial Iranian Air Force F-86F Sabre in the colours of the IIAF Golden Crown aerobatic team. *(Photos: Tim McLelland collection)*

convert onto the F-104 Starfighter. The last AM F-86K was withdrawn from service in July 1973.

Japan

Towards the end of 1953, the former wartime Allied nations (but not the USSR) agreed to allow Japan to re-equip its military forces, and it was agreed that F-86Fs would be supplied to the Japan Air Self Defense Force (JASDF). In 1954, the F-86F was selected to be the standard fighter of the JASDF, with Sabres coming from USAF surplus stocks, although eventually they would be assembled in Japan under a licence agreement, by Mitsubishi, based at Nagoya. Between December 1955 and 1956, the JASDF received 29 former USAF F-86F-25 and F-86F-30 aircraft. JASDF serials were 52-7401 to 7410 and 62-7411 to 7430. The first JASDF Wing was activated in October 1956 at Hamamatsu with 68 T-33A trainers and some 20 F-86Fs. A total of 135 former USAF F-86Fs were delivered to the JASDF between 1956 and early 1957. Most of these were Korean War veterans that were eventually refurbished and modified to F-86F-40 standard, although the final 45 aircraft were never flown and eventually returned to the USA, largely because of a shortage of Japanese pilots. Mitsubishi built some 300 F-86F-40s under licence between 1956 and 1961. The JASDF was the first customer for the F-86F-40-NA, receiving its first examples in 1956. In December 1961, Mitsubishi modified 18 surplus USAF F-86F-25 and F-86F-30 aircraft to RF-86F configuration by installing camera equipment (resulting in a modified forward fuselage shape with a bulged fuselage fairings). These were delivered to the 501st Hikotai, where they remained in service until 1979 when they were replaced by RF-4E Phantoms. In all, some 480 F-86Fs were flown by the JASDF, and the last Japanese F-86F (63-7497) made its final flight on 15 March 1982. Many JASDF Sabres were eventually returned to the USA under the

Italian Air Force F-86E Sabres in early unpainted finish and later camouflage colours. *(Photos: Tim McLelland collection)*

JASDF F-86F and F-86D Sabres in standard squadron markings, and with the Blue Impulse aerobatic team. *(Photos: Tim McLelland collection)*

Republic of Korea Air Force F-86F Sabres, still in service during 1977. *(Photo: Karl Hammer)*

Royal Malaysian Air Force CAC (Commonwealth Aircraft Corporation) Sabre Mk.32 FM1983. *(Photo: Key Collection)*

terms of the MAP agreement with which they had been supplied.

Korea

The Republic of Korea Air Force (RoKAF) obtained its first Sabres during 1955 when five F-86Fs were officially handed over on 20 June. Korea eventually received 85 former USAF F-86F-25 and F-86F-30 fighters, deliveries being made from June 1955 until June 1956. The Sabres replaced F-51D Mustang fighters that equipped the RoKAF's 10th Wing. During 1958, 27 additional F-86Fs and ten RF-86F reconnaissance aircraft were also delivered, and many of the RoKAF Sabres were retrofitted with the 'F-40' wing, incorporating extended tips and slats. Many were modified to carry the AIM-9 Sidewinder air-to-air missile. The RoKAF's Sabres began to be replaced in 1965 when the first Northrop F-5s were delivered, although at least three F-86Fs remained in use until 1987.

Malaysia

Australia presented ten Sabres to the Royal Malaysian Air Force (Tentera Udara Diraja Malaysia) in 1969, together with spares and technical support, plus training personnel. A new unit, No.11 (Cobra) Squadron, was formed for the Sabres, at Butterworth. Deliveries began in August 1969 and after completion of the ten-aircraft transfer, an additional six were delivered, together with a single airframe to act as a ground-based trainer. Another ground trainer was supplied in February 1974. No.12 (Lightning) Squadron eventually assumed Sabre operations from No.11 Squadron, and following the arrival of F-5 fighters during April 1976, the Sabres were phased out. Most of the aircraft remained in Malaysia as ground training airframes, although five were transferred to Indonesia during July 1976.

Netherlands

The Koninklijke Luchtmacht (KLu) operated 57 NAA-built F-86Ks, all of which were delivered by sea — the first being on the USS *Tripoli* — from October 1955 until April 1956. They were assigned to Nos. 700, 701 and 702 Squadrons. During 1957, these aircraft were supplemented by six F-86Ks assembled in Italy by Fiat. Sixteen F-86Ks were ultimately destroyed by accidents while in service, and eight machines were returned to Italy in 1963. The Dutch F-86Ks were finally replaced by F-104G Starfighters during the mid-1960s, with official withdrawal taking place on 31 October 1964. After the aircraft were removed from service, most examples of the F-86K were scrapped, but 54-1305 (code Q-305) survived this process and remains on display at the Royal Netherlands Air Force museum at Soesterberg.

Norway

The Royal Norwegian Air Force took delivery of its first Sabres in 1957 when the initial F-86Fs arrived in March, enabling the replacement of F-84G Thunderjets to begin. By the end of that year some 30 Sabres had been delivered, and the remainder of the fleet of 90 aircraft was supplied to Norway by the following May. 332 Skvadron based at Rygge was the first F-86 unit, followed by 331, 334, 336 and finally 338 Skvadron at Orland. During June 1960 a batch of six F-86F attrition

F-86K Sabres, operated by the Royal Netherlands Air Force (Koninklijke Luchtmacht) from 1955 until 1964. *(Photos: Tim McLelland collection)*

replacements arrived, followed by another 19 aircraft in January 1961, these being transported from the US by sea. In September 1955 the first F-86Ks arrived, although one was lost during acceptance trials in the US, and another four were destroyed in a hangar fire in March 1956. Replacements (four Fiat-built aircraft) arrived in June. First unit to form was 337 Skvadron at Gardermoen, followed by 339 Skvadron. These units merged with 332 and 334 Skvadrons in September 1963, When the first F-104 Starfighters arrived in April 1963, the F-86Fs began to be withdrawn, while more were replaced by F-5s (and some of the F-86F units had already converted onto the F-86K). Most of the F-86Fs were withdrawn by 1966, with many being refurbished for further MAP distribution to countries such as Portugal. The last of the F-86K fleet was withdrawn on 15 July 1967 and the majority were eventually scrapped.

Pakistan

Pakistan received the first of 120 F-86F Sabres in 1954, most of these aircraft being F-86F-35s from existing USAF stocks, although some were also supplied from a later F-86F-40-NA block that was produced by North American specifically for exports. Many of the F-86F-35s were modified to F-86F-40 standard before being delivered to Pakistan, although a few remained unmodified as F-86F-35s throughout their service life. Pakistan's Sabres were key participants in the 17-day war with India in 1965, fought over the status of Kashmir. Although the Sabre could no longer compete with new supersonic fighters, the F-86Fs performed well. The top Pakistani ace of the conflict was Wing Commander Mohammed Mahmood Alam, who ended the conflict with a total of 11 kills. Remarkably, only seven Sabres were recorded as being lost in air combat during the 1965 conflict. Pakistan's F-86Fs saw further action during the

1971 war with India, and the Sabres accounted for a large proportion of the PAF's 141 aerial victory claims. Following the first conflict, Pakistan had attempted to obtain more Sabres, but with UN pressure to prevent sales to either India or Pakistan, a deal was struck with Iran to acquire a fleet of 90 Canadair Sabres that had been withdrawn from use by the Luftwaffe. Iran successfully circumvented the UN and duly supplied the Sabres to Pakistan, and it was mostly aircraft from this order that participated in the 1971 war, many of the original F-86Fs having already been withdrawn. The last of Pakistan's Sabres were retired in 1980, following a series of fatigue-related accidents. Most of the surviving fleet was placed in long-term storage pending possible future use but all of the Sabres were eventually abandoned.

Peru

The Peruvian Air Force (Fuerza Aérea del Perú) received a batch of 12 former USAF F-86F-25s beginning in September 1955. Two aircraft were lost in accidents and a batch of attrition replacements was supplied from USAF stocks at Davis-Monthan AFB, bringing the FAP fleet to a total of 15 by 1960. Attrition losses were significant, and at least nine had been lost in accidents by December 1963. One of the primary causes was the appearance of wing spar cracks caused chiefly by excessive manoeuvring. This was a result of Sabre pilots competing with the more capable Hunters that were operated by other FAP squadrons. The surviving Sabres soldiered on for many years, largely because of an inability to obtain further MAP aircraft from the US. Finally, Sukhoi Su-22s were delivered in 1976 and this enabled the last of the Sabres to be retired.

Philippines

The Philippine Air Force (Hukbong Himpapawid ng Pilipinas) received a fleet of F-86F-25, F-86F-30 and F-86F-35 aircraft beginning in 1957. An initial batch of four was followed by 30 machines, and another 15 during June 1958. Further Sabres arrived in 1959 and even more in 1962 when a small number were obtained from Spain. The aircraft equipped the 6th and 7th Tactical Fighter Squadrons of the 5th Fighter Wing, and the 8th and 9th Tactical Fighter Squadrons of the 6th Fighter Wing. Many of the F-86Fs were eventually upgraded to F-86F-40 standard. The Sabres were replaced by Northrop F-5s beginning in 1966 and the last PAF F-86Fs were withdrawn in 1978, when the remaining aircraft (assigned to a reserve squadron) were withdrawn.

Portugal

The Portuguese Air Force (Forca Aerea Portuguesa) acquired 65 F-86Fs from former USAF stocks beginning in 1958. An initial batch of 33 was followed by 30 more in 1959, and a final pair in 1961, most of the aircraft being supplied by Fiat in Italy, where the aircraft had been refurbished. Six former Norwegian aircraft were supplied as spares sources, together with three from Saudi Arabia. With serials 5301 to 5365, some of the Sabres saw active service in Angola, and by the late 1970s only six aircraft remained in use, the majority having succumbed to fatigue problems, flying accidents or 'combat losses' (mostly in the form of sabotage attacks as no flying losses were recorded). It wasn't until 31 July 1980 that they were finally withdrawn, following the delivery of T-38s from the US.

Saudi Arabia

The fledgling Royal Saudi Air Force (Al Quwwat Al-Jawwiya Assa'udiaya) received the first of 16 F-86F-40s during September 1957, although they were not officially transferred to RSAF control until 1961. Operating the Sabres proved to be difficult, not least because Saudi Arabia didn't have the necessary infrastructure with which to overhaul or maintain the aircraft, and they were routinely sent overseas (usually to Germany) for attention. The fleet remained in use however, being joined by a further 30 machines in 1967. During 1969 some aircraft saw action over the border with Yemen, following the British withdrawal from the region. When F-5s began to arrive in 1971, the Sabres were gradually withdrawn and the last survivors were retired in 1977, many being simply dumped on the perimeter of their former operating base at Dhahran, where their remains can still be found.

South Africa

A fleet of 18 USAF F-86Fs was loaned to the South African Air Force (SAAF) in January

F-86F and F-86K Sabres, supplied to Norway from 1957 onwards. ***(Photos: Tim McLelland collection)***

1953, replacing No.2 Squadron's F-51D Mustangs that had been deployed to Korea as part of the USAF's 18th Fighter Bomber Wing. No.2 Squadron flew 2,032 sorties in Korea until fighting ended in July 1953. The Sabres were then returned to the US, but in 1954 the Canadair Sabre was selected to replace the SAAF's Vampire fleet, and some 34 Sabre Mk.6s were purchased, the first arriving by sea in August 1956. Nos. 1 and 2 Squadrons operated the Sabres from their base at Waterkloof. They remained active until January 1981 when most of the surviving aircraft were scrapped, although ten were sold to Flight Systems in the US. These Sabres were never flown and after years of open storage at Mojave, they were re-sold to civilian buyers.

Spain

Two F-86F-25s arrived in Spain on 30 June 1955, becoming the first Sabres to join the Spanish Air Force (Ejército del Aire). Both were USAF aircraft formerly with the 86th FBW in Germany. A further five Sabres arrived in September and another 125 aircraft came from MAP reserves held at Châteauroux in France. A total of 270 F-86Fs were ultimately delivered to Spain and all were gradually modernised to F-86F-40 standard. During the 1960s, many of the Sabres were modified to operate the AIM-9 Sidewinder missile and in 1962 a number were returned to USAF control for re-distribution to other nations as part of the MAP system. The gradual run-down of the Sabre fleet then began as new aircraft (including the F-104 Starfighter) came into service. However, it

An F-86F-35-NA shortly after delivery to Pakistan. *(Photo: Key Collection)*

One of 12 F-86F-25-NAs supplied to the Peruvian Air Force (Fuerza Aérea del Perú) during 1955. *(Photo: Tim McLelland collection)*

Philippine Air Force (Hukbong Himpapawid ng Pilipinas) F-86F-25-NA, soon after delivery in 1957. *(Photo: Tim McLelland collection)*

wasn't until December 1972 that the last F-86 mission was flown, with the final EdA Sabre unit (Ala 41) disbanding at the end of that month.

Taiwan

Although the USAF and RCAF were the major users of the Sabre, the Republic of China Air Force (RoCAF) wasn't too far behind, having acquired more than 500 examples in total. Beginning in 1954, some 320 F-86Fs and seven RF-86Fs were delivered, although more F-86Fs followed, together with a number of F-86D variants. The RoCAF Sabres were involved in various incidents, including a reconnaissance mission over China during January 1956, resulting in the aircraft being impounded in Hong Kong. Two Sabres intercepted a BOAC Comet off Taiwan during January 1959, and in July of that year three Sabres engaged MiG-15s over the Formosa

Portuguese Air Force (Forca Aérea Portuguesa) F-86F Sabres towards the end of their operational service life, during the 1970s. *(Photo: Tim McLelland collection)*

Royal Saudi Air Force (Al Quwwat Al-Jawwiya Assa'udiaya) F-86F Sabres during the late 1960s. *(Photo: Tim McLelland collection)*

F-86F Sabres from No.2 Squadron, South African Air Force in early and late colour schemes. *(Photos: Tim McLelland collection)*

Spanish Air Force (Ejército del Aire) F-86F-25-NA Sabre, circa 1970. *(Photo: Tim McLelland collection)*

Republic of China Air Force F-86F Sabres at Nellis AFB during training with the USAF prior to delivery. *(Photo: D. Moser)*

Straits, resulting in the downing of two MiGs. From 1958 when more open conflict began, the Sabres were routinely involved in interceptions, most aircraft being equipped with Sidewinder missiles. Further action continued after hostilities ended, with four Sabres being intercepted by MiG-17s during February 1960. From 1959 the F-86Fs were partially replaced by a batch of F-86Ds, although the majority of the F-86Fs remained in use until the F-104 and F-5 came into service. The last of the Sabres were finally retired during April 1971 and most were eventually destroyed, although some were transferred to the US Navy for use as spares for the QF-86 drone programme.

Turkish Air Force (Türk Hava Kuvvetleri) F-86E(M) Canadair Sabre, during 1957. *(Photo: Tim McLelland collection)*

Thailand

Although the USA regarded Thailand as an important nation in terms of controlling communist expansion, it was not viewed as an urgent case in terms of military support. Thus, it wasn't until 1960 that the first Sabres arrived in Thailand, after an initial 20 F-86F-30 airframes were converted to F-86F-40 standard and shipped to Thailand under a MAP agreement. The aircraft arrived in October, enabling F-84s and F8F-1 Bearcats to be replaced. A second batch of F-86Fs arrived in March 1962, and additional aircraft were eventually acquired as attrition replacements, these coming from various sources including Norway and Saudi Arabia. In 1964 a batch of 20 F-86L all-weather interceptors came into service, all being former US Air National Guard machines, and as such Thailand was the only nation outside the US to operate this variant. Northrop F-5A fighters began to arrive in 1966 and this enabled the F-86Fs to slowly be withdrawn, although it wasn't until 1972 that the last aircraft were retired, having been replaced by A-37s. The F-86L

Venezuelan F-86F Sabres at McClellan AFB in California prior to delivery, February 1967. *(Photo: Bob Burns)*

Surviving F-86K at the Museo Aeronautico de Maracay. *(Photo: Aeroprints.com)*

▲ ► A series of rare colour photographs from the Yugoslavian Air Force, illustrating former Royal Air Force Canadair Sabre Mk.4s that were delivered in 1967. *(Photos: Tim McLelland collection)*

variants remained active until 1976 when they were replaced by F-5Es.

Tunisia

A batch of 12 F-86F-40s was delivered to Tunisia during 1969, all being former JASDF machines that had been returned to the US for storage and possible refurbishment. The aircraft were shipped in two batches of six, the second delivery being completed on 17 November. Based at Sidi Ahmed Air Base with No.11 Squadron, they enjoyed a relatively brief service life, being supplemented and eventually replaced by Italian MB-326Ks.

Turkey

The Turkish Air Force (Türk Hava Kuvvetleri) received 107 Canadair Sabres beginning in June 1954. All of these were modified to F-86E(M) standard, complete with '6-3' wings. The last of the order (two having been lost during delivery) arrived in 1956. First squadron to operate the Sabre was 141 Filo, followed by 142 Filo. It is believed that some Royal Netherlands Air Force F-86Ks were to have been transferred to Turkey but no such development occurred, and by 1960 some 80 Sabres were still in use, many having been lost in accidents. Deliveries of F-104 Starfighters and F-5 'Freedom Fighters' enabled replacement of the Sabres to begin in 1964, and the type was finally retired late in 1968.

Venezuela

A small batch of just seven F-86Fs was delivered to Venezuela during August 1956, as part of a MAP agreement to supply the country with Sabres, in order to replace a fleet of elderly Vampire fighters. Six more Sabres arrived in October and another eight in February 1957. All of these were assigned to Escuadrón de Caza 36, at Mariscal Sucre. Some of these Sabres were employed during an attempted revolution early in 1958, with four Sabres making strafing attacks on the Presidential Palace, the Ministry of Defence and National Security Headquarters. The ensuing political and military chaos had direct effects on Venezuela's air force, and a combination of accidents and a shortage of resources led to the Sabre fleet rapidly diminishing until only six aircraft were still airworthy by late 1958. However, in 1965 an agreement was made to purchase 78 former Luftwaffe F-86K Sabres, although some aircraft were to be used only as spares sources (and four were impounded during delivery). Equipping Escuadrón de Caza 34 and 35, they also suffered from a shortage of maintenance and spare parts support, and by 1969 most of the fleet was no longer airworthy. All of the Sabres were withdrawn by 1974, nine F-86Fs going to the Bolivian Air Force, and four F-86Ks to Honduras.

Yugoslavia

As part of MAP arrangements, Yugoslavia was allocated a fleet of former Royal Air Force Canadair Sabre Mk.4s, all modified to F-86E(M) standard with unslatted '6-3' wings. Refurbishment was undertaken by a number of companies, at Stansted, Dunsfold, Gatwick, Speke and Merryfield. Deliveries began in May 1956 although they didn't start to arrive in substantial deliveries until May 1957, and by the end of that year some 37 Sabres were in service. By this stage, relations with the Soviet Union had improved and Yugoslavia announced that all military aid from the USA would end. Deliveries of Sabres concluded with the 43rd aircraft.

However, the political situation soon changed and the US agreed to supply a further 78 former RAF Sabres in 1959, together with 130 ex-USAF F-86Ds. Some of the latter variants were modified in service to operate in the reconnaissance role (IF-86D), with three K-24 cameras replacing the standard Mighty Mouse rocket pack. The gradual development of an indigenous aircraft industry led to the introduction of the Galeb and Jastreb, and as these aircraft came into service the F-86E fleet was gradually withdrawn, the last examples being retired in 1971. The F-86D fleet remained in use until the end of 1974. Four were sold to Honduras during 1976. ❖

THE BRITISH INTERLUDE

The Sabre joins the ranks of the Royal Air Force

Sabres from No.92 Squadron, RAF, high over the Yorkshire coast. *(Photo: Key Collection)*

Canadair Sabres fresh from the production line, during their long transatlantic deployment to the United Kingdom. *(Photos: Tim McLelland collection)*

The British government (and particularly the Air Ministry) had followed development of the Sabre with great interest, from the very beginning of the project. English Electric's test pilot Roland Beamont test-flew the aircraft during a visit to the USA in May 1948 and even with a 4,000lb-thrust engine, the second prototype XP-86 certainly impressed him. He reported that the aircraft handled remarkably well, achieved excellent speeds and altitudes, and had a well-laid-out cockpit that was a joy to fly in. A serving Royal Air Force pilot, Flight Lieutenant Paddy Harbison, subsequently became the next 'Brit' to fly the Sabre, after becoming an exchange officer with the 1st Fighter Group at March AFB in California. He too was greatly impressed by the aircraft and when he returned to the UK during the summer of 1950, he shared his enthusiasm with his RAF colleagues and Air Force chiefs. However, few people in the UK were convinced that either he or Beamont were being entirely honest about the Sabre's capabilities. After all, the RAF had the Meteor and the Vampire and both aircraft were regarded as being at the very forefront of jet fighter design. It seemed likely that the American experience must have been a triumph of presentation over capability. However, this view quickly changed when the Korean War began. The Meteor saw service in theatre with the Royal Australian Air Force and the Meteor pilots soon discovered that the jet was no match for the MiGs that roamed the skies over Korea. The hapless Meteor was quickly shifted from the role of a fighter to that of a ground attack aircraft, and the USAF was left to take on the MiGs with the fast and agile F-86 Sabre. The RAF reluctantly learned the lessons of Korea and realised that a new swept-wing fighter was needed – and needed soon. Supermarine's Swift was on the proverbial horizon as was Hawker's Hunter, but in the shorter term there was no prospect of a new swept-wing fighter being produced in Britain. The only means of getting one would be to buy one from overseas; indeed the only aircraft that could possibly give the RAF what it needed was the F-86 Sabre. However, on 13 September 1950 the Chief of the Air Staff (CAS) Sir John Slessor obtained a briefing on Canada's Avro CF-100 all-weather fighter, as a potential candidate to meet the RAF's Specfication F.4/48 for such an aeroplane. In response, the Ministry of Defence outlined to Slessor all of Canada's aircraft projects, including the licence-production of F-86 Sabres. Slessor wasn't particularly interested in the Sabre, believing that an 'off the shelf' purchase of an existing aircraft was unnecessary when the Swift and Hunter would be available to the RAF in due course. The problem with this outlook was that the development of British fighters would take time, and of course there was no guarantee that either of these projects would create a viable combat aircraft. By comparison, the Sabre already existed and it was demonstrably capable of providing the performance that the RAF required. Slessor remained unimpressed but in October 1950 he flew to Canada to tour aircraft production facilities and to see precisely what was on offer. Canada's extensive, high-quality facilities

were sufficient to change Slessor's view and he quickly accepted that the F-86 was perhaps not such a crazy idea. It was clear that Canada had the capability and capacity to manufacture the Sabre quickly, and provide the RAF with a very capable jet fighter far faster than any British manufacturer ever could. His conclusion was that the "F-86 looks like being far the earliest answer to our most unpleasant problem." Meanwhile, the Air Standardisation Co-ordination Committee Combined Test Project Agreement had been signed on 14 September. This rather unwieldy title outlined an arrangement that would enable Britain to evaluate the Sabre more extensively, without any interference from commercial and industrial interests (indeed, Britain's aircraft manufacturers were specifically excluded from any access to the aircraft). Two F-86As were delivered to RAF West Raynham on 14 October 1950 and temporarily assigned to the Central Fighter Establishment.

During their stay at West Raynham, the Sabres were investigated thoroughly, with key areas being explored in detail, these being general handling and performance, engine handling and performance, and tactical operations. As part of this latter phase the Sabres were flown against Meteor fighters and B-29 bombers, in low, medium and high-level combat exercises. The Sabre's direct comparison with the Meteor was something of a revelation as although the Meteor performed well, the Sabre had a better rate of climb, a better rate of roll, a faster level speed and a faster dive speed. In fact the Sabre was judged to be far superior to the Meteor in every practical aspect and was, therefore a much better fighter aircraft than anything else available at that time. The only possible shortfall was the Sabre's machine gun armament, which was undoubtedly inferior to the cannon armament fitted to the Meteor. By March 1951 the evaluation flying at West Raynham was complete and the Sabres went to Boscombe Down where the A&AEE test pilots conducted further handling tests and also performed some weapon suitability exercises together with instrument error calibration and engine thrust research. The pilots agreed with the CFE's findings that the Sabre was an excellent aircraft, although they believed that the aileron surfaces didn't profile sufficient 'feel' through the pilot's controls and that at low speed they were unnecessarily sensitive. Rather oddly, they also commented that the Sabre's cockpit layout was poor, and was somewhat confusing when compared to British aeroplanes. This was totally at odds

with the views expressed by Roland Beamont. One of the Sabres then went to Farnborough where the aircraft's lateral stability was investigated, followed by a closer look at its rudder trim tab and its effectiveness. It was also examined as part of a profile-drag analysis, to compare with the Supermarine and Hawker fighter designs that were being developed. But the Sabre's stay at Farnborough came to a premature end on 14 August 1952 when it crashed following an 'elevator runaway' incident. The pilot ejected safely, and the second Sabre was duly sent to Farnborough to continue testing. It was grounded on arrival for rectification of an aileron trim problem and stayed in a RAE hangar until January, but after repair a number of other minor faults had arisen requiring another lengthy stay on the ground. When spare parts were finally obtained, they were found to be the wrong type for this particular variant and so it wasn't until early March 1953 that the aircraft flew again. After just three days it suffered hydraulic failure and it wasn't until June that flying resumed, some 13 hours being completed before the aircraft was grounded again for inspection. It returned to flying in February 1954 when a series of flights were conducted to investigate ways in which the Sabre's high-speed performance could be improved. As part of these tests the wing leading edge slats were fixed in a retracted position and sealed smooth, after which vortex generators were tested followed by wing fences, of various sizes and at different positions on the wings. The vortex generators reduced wing drop above Mach 0.92 and increased longitudinal stability, whereas the wing fences delayed the aircraft's tendency to pitch up, at the expense of a slight reduction in overall performance. Finally, a leading-edge extension was fitted to each wing, created by fixing the outer two-thirds of the leading-edge slats in the two-thirds extended position. This improved the nose-up pitching tendency at Mach 0.8 but had no great effect by the time the aircraft reached Mach 0.92. Much of this testing was a repetition of work that was being conducted by the manufacturer (NAA) but it provided useful independent data for the RAE, and served to confirm every detail of the Sabre's performance. Because the second loaned aeroplane had spent so much time grounded, two extensions to the loan agreement were made and it wasn't until November 1954 that the aircraft was finally flown back to Burtonwood and returned to the USAF.

Slessor's agreement to procure the Sabre for the RAF didn't immediately result in a

Sabres at RAF Kinloss after completing their flight across the Atlantic. ***(Photo: Key Collection)***

A quartet of F-86s from the RAF's Sabre Conversion Unit, near RAF Wildenrath in Germany during 1953. *(Photo: Key Collection)*

Sabre XB543 was used by the Central Fighter Establishment to establish the aerodynamic effects of camouflage paint on the aircraft's performance. This led to the decision to apply camouflage to all of the RAF's Sabres. *(Photo: Tim McLelland collection)*

purchase, not least because there was some concern that Britain could barely afford them. Initially, it was expected that US Military Aid would finance the project, but any hopes that the USA would buy the aeroplanes for Britain were thwarted in October 1950 when the British Joint Services Mission learned from US officials that Military Aid was to be provided for the acquisition of ground attack aircraft, only and that the design and manufacture of fighters should be undertaken by the European NATO members themselves. Although the Sabre was ostensibly a fighter-interceptor, it was accepted that like many other contemporary fighter designs, it also had a good ground attack capability, but the US Government regarded it as a fighter, and so there seemed to be no prospect of procuring the aircraft unless it was paid for by the British taxpayer. Slessor continued to plan for a purchase, and outlined a requirement for 380 Sabres to equip six squadrons, each with 22 aircraft and a three-month war reserve fleet. He stated that it would be at least two years before so much as one squadron in the RAF would be equipped "with a type that is not outclassed by the MiG 15." He advised the Canadian and American governments that the RAF would require 300 Sabres (rather fewer than he had originally proposed) and the Air Ministry sought clarification from Washington as to precisely what their definition of "tactical aircraft" actually was. The response was that it effectively meant fighter-bombers, light bombers and tactical reconnaissance aircraft, so the RAF would not be able to use the aircraft as a fighter if it was purchased through MDAP (Mutual Defense Assistance Program) funding. Canada confirmed that Sabres could be manufactured and delivered quickly within MDAP funding arrangements but if the RAF accepted an order, it would have to agree to not use the aircraft in the fighter role. Despite these setbacks, the British government supported an application from the Air Staff for Slessor's 300 aircraft (and a larger plan for up to 402 aircraft) but when this was submitted on 30 October 1950 it was refused on the grounds that it contravened US policy. Slessor was expecting this response and stated that if the Treasury purchased the aircraft, the RAF could obviously use the Sabres however British policy required. He added that North American could supply Sabres at $200,000 per aircraft, whereas Canadair could offer a price tag of $323,000. Thus an outright purchase from NAA of the F-86E would be the best option for Britain. Washington subsequently informed London that NAA simply didn't have the production capacity to build Sabres for the RAF quickly, meaning any purchase would have to be placed with Canadair, but many components could be supplied directly from US companies. These could be financed by MDAP funding, thereby making the purchase less expensive without contravening US government policy. The US government wanted to help Britain as best it could but Slessor remained unmoved, stating "It hardly seems wise that the US should confine themselves under MDAP to supply of fighter-bombers which we and even France

An unusual view of four Sabres completing a loop over Yorkshire. It illustrates the contrasting underside colours applied to the camouflaged Sabre, with two aircraft featuring a silver finish while two more use a PRU blue. *(Photo: Key Collection)*

can produce, and withhold high-performance interceptors which at present we cannot." He subsequently suggested that if the Sabres were assigned to overseas tactical squadrons within the RAF, it might be possible to justify MDAP funding, even if the aircraft were used as fighters once they were acquired. Eventually an agreement was made on this basis. The US accepted that MDAP funding could cover the purchase of Sabres to equip RAF overseas squadrons, and that they would be used to provide 'top cover' for the RAF's existing Vampire and Venom ground attack aircraft. Of course, this effectively meant that the Sabres would be used as fighters, but their incorporation into a tactical role was enough to sufficiently cloud the issue and enable funding to be made available. On 2 October 1951 the Canadian government approved the proposed deal and funding for 395 Sabres was approved by the US government in February 1952.

After negotiation it was agreed that 370 Sabres would be produced for the RAF and all of the aircraft would be Mk.4 variants, apart from three which would be F-86Es with J47 engines. By November 1952 the American attitude on the supply of fighters had also changed slightly, and the Air Ministry was advised that MDAP would now fund the supply a further batch of 60 aircraft, these being Canadair Sabre Mk.4 variants that were now surplus to requirements. Crucially, it was agreed that they could be supplied directly to Fighter Command and that some additional aeroplanes could be transferred from the tactical squadrons in Germany, to form three fighter squadrons, each with 22 aircraft. By the middle of the following year the RAF's intentions had changed and plans were made for just two Sabre squadrons to be formed in the UK, beginning in September of that year. They were to remain active until March 1955 when it was estimated that Hunter fighters would be coming into RAF service. However, the RAF's procurement plans were affected by a growing shortage of Sabres within the RCAF squadrons in Germany. The RCAF asked if Sabres destined for the RAF could be loaned so that its re-equipment plans could continue at full strength. Despite the obvious fact that the RAF needed the Sabres just as quickly as Canada, it was agreed that 60 aircraft would be diverted to the RCAF until Canadair's production schedule could catch up, at which stage they would be transferred back to the RAF. The loan was very short-term and as agreed, the aircraft were withdrawn from Canadian service by December 1953 and ferried to the UK. They were inspected by Airwork before being placed in storage at Kemble, pending delivery to operational units. Meanwhile, plans had been made to receive the main fleet of Sabres and rather than take the risky and laborious step of having each aircraft shipped across the Atlantic, the RAF decided to fly them from Canada. The RCAF had flown its aircraft across to Germany (via the UK) and had encountered no significant problems, so it seemed logical to follow the same procedure. A final decision was made on 10 July 1952 and with 60 aircraft being allocated to the RCAF loan, some 370 Sabres would require ferrying across the Atlantic under Operation Becher's Brook. The first task was to train three RAF pilots to fly the Sabre, and the RCAF agreed to provide the training at No.1 Operational Training Unit based at

Chatham, New Brunswick. The three pilots (from No.1 Overseas Ferry Unit) left for Canada during August and after converting onto the aircraft, they were tasked with the ferrying of three examples that would be used for initial familiarisation in the UK. While the pilots were training, RAF ground crews were instructed on the Sabre at RAF North Luffenham in Rutland – already an active RCAF Sabre base. The three Sabre F.Mk.2s departed Saint-Hubert in Canada on 28 September 1952, and arrived at Prestwick on 4 October, after which they made the short hop to North Luffenham on the 10th. Although they arrived with RCAF serials, they were soon repainted as XB530, XB531 and XB532 and immediately allocated to RAF ferry pilot training with No.1 OFU. Training each pilot took approximately two weeks and with a ground school and ten flying hours, each ferry pilot was then ready to head for Canada to conduct additional training (including another 15 hours of flying) as well as some very important survival training. Some 60 pilots — all with at least 400 hours of jet flying experience — were also temporarily transferred from 2 TAF in Germany to take part in the ferry exercise, so that sufficient crews would be available for the major task at hand.

When each Sabre was completed by Canadair, they were test-flown and transferred to Bagotville by RAF pilots. Final maintenance was conducted there and then each aircraft was handed to No.1 OFU for a few hours of preparatory flying, to ensure that the aircraft was free of any potential problems. Airborne servicing teams were gathered in the UK and flown to Canada so that they could accompany the Sabres on their long journey in a Hastings transport, one team flying ahead of each ferry 'package' while the other followed, with some additional crew assigned to the care of the Hastings transport itself. The first of the Becher's Brook ferry flights began on 9 December 1953, comprising nine Sabres, rather than the proposed full 'package' of 30 aircraft. A full-sized servicing crew was assigned to the exercise so that as many personnel as possible could gain experience. After leaving Bagotville, the aircraft routed via Goose Bay, Bluie West One, Keflavik and finally Prestwick in Scotland. Becher's Brook 1 proceeded without any significant problems until the very end of the exercise, when XB534 crashed whilst on final approach to Prestwick, the pilot being killed in the accident. The remaining eight aircraft finally arrived at RAF Abingdon on 2 January 1953, and the Sabres were officially handed over by the Canadian High Commissioner, who read a message from the Canadian Minister of Defence. It said; "This ceremony marks the arrival and delivery of the first of the F-86E Sabres provided to the Royal Air Force by Canada. The RAF has already received three aircraft from us, which were flown over in October by RAF pilots, but these were advanced out of our own supply. A little more than a year ago, Mr. Arthur Henderson, at that time the Secretary of State for Air, and Marshal of the RAF Sir John Slessor, then Chief of the Air Staff of the RAF, discussed with Air Marshal Curtis, CAS of the RCAF, and myself the possibility of obtaining Sabre fighters to

Four Sabres wearing the yellow and red markings of No.92 Squadron, based at RAF Linton-on-Ouse. ***(Photo: Key Collection)***

supplement the air defences in Britain. At about the same time, approaches were made to the United States. The result was an arrangement whereby the United States at their expense provided the engines and other components to be put into aircraft produced by Canadair Ltd., and paid for by Canada, to be delivered for use by the RAF. This was a three-way partnership for our common defence. Production has proceeded so satisfactorily that it has been possible to advance the delivery dates originally proposed so that they are some six months in advance of the original target date. We are now beginning the regular delivery of so many each week and month until the total is completed. The exact number of aircraft has not been announced, but it is between 300 and 400 and I can tell you that it is closer to 400 than to 300. This arrangement represents by far the largest single act of military assistance given by Canada to the United Kingdom since the war. It represents, in the part contributed by Canada alone, a total of about $100 million. We are glad to do this because it is part of our common defence".

Despite the tragic end to Becher's Brook One (the crash being unrelated to the ferry process), the RAF proceeded with Becher's Brook Two and Three. Encouraged by the success of these flights, Becher's Brook Four (which began in March 1953) became a 'double' exercise, and when the first gaggle of 32 Sabres arrived at each staging post, the support crews were flown back to the previous point to support a second wave of another 32 aircraft. Some serviceability issues arose but despite minor problems, 60 Sabres were delivered to Abingdon in just four days through this process. The ferry flights continued and by May 1954 a total of 372 aircraft had crossed the Atlantic, and Operation Becher's Brook was over. With the Sabres delivered, the RAF now had to begin converting fighter pilots onto the type, and planning for this process had been under way for some time. Pilots assigned to the Sabre were initially sent to the USA where they underwent standard USAF flight training on the F-84 Thunderjet and the F-86, and although this arrangement ensured that the pilots gained very thorough training, it was an expensive and inconvenient procedure. From late March 1953, No.147 Squadron at Abingdon began to undertake Sabre training, and that June the task transferred to Wildenrath in Germany. The plan was for the Germany-based squadrons to be trained at Wildenrath, after which Sabres would be assigned to No.229 Operational Conversion Unit at Chivenor, so that British fighter pilots could convert onto the Sabre there. The Sabre Conversion Flight was duly formed at Wildenrath and from June 1954 the training task was undertaken by the OCU at Chivenor. The first operational RAF squadron to receive the Sabre was No.67 based at Wildenrath. After receiving aircraft directly from the Becher's Brook ferry flights, the unit began flying operational sorties in May 1953. No.3 Squadron then began to re-equip with Sabres

Sabres from No.112 Squadron during a sortie from their home base at Brüggen in Germany. *(Photo: Key Collection)*

and No. 93 Squadron began to receive Sabres in March 1954. Fighter Command took delivery of the second batch of Sabres towards the end of 1953 and in December No.66 Squadron re-equipped with the type, followed by No.92 Squadron in February 1954. Both units were based at Linton-on-Ouse in Yorkshire and had previously operated the Meteor. As expected, the Sabre proved to be an excellent aircraft and one that was liked by all those who flew it. A variety of aerobatic teams appeared, all prompted by the sheer enthusiasm of the squadrons that were lucky enough to fly the sleek and manoeuvrable fighter. It was a major progression from the rather pedestrian Vampire and Meteor, and one that enabled the RAF to finally realise the potential of the jet engine. The Sabre's time with the RAF was short but intentionally so, as the aircraft had never been regarded as anything other than a 'stop gap' until the Hunter entered service. But when the Hunter F.Mk.1 first joined the ranks of the Air Force, it was less than perfect and it wasn't until the Hunter F.Mk.4 began to appear that the Sabre finally had a successor. During the spring of 1956 the Sabres based at Linton-on-Ouse were replaced by Hunters and by the summer the type had also been withdrawn from Germany, the last aircraft to leave being XB670 of No.3 Squadron.

Plans to withdraw the Sabre actually began in July 1953 when the Air Staff first discussed how it would eventually be replaced by the Hunter. It was proposed that the Sabres should be supplanted on a one-for-one basis and funded in the same way by the Military Assistance Program (MAP). During August it was agreed that 220 Sabres could be made available for return to the USA, all overhauled and handed back in airworthy condition. In exchange for these, Britain could receive Hunters. Of course, the ownership of the Sabres was split between the USA and Canada and there was a great deal of discussion as to how they should be

N
XB956
V

disposed of. Britain favoured the transfer of the aircraft to European nations, particularly Denmark, the Netherlands, Belgium or Norway, but Italy and Yugoslavia were also identified as secondary choices. Agreement was eventually made with Canada to transfer complete ownership of the Sabres to the USA, and despite a lot of discussion, it was effectively the US that finally dictated that the Sabres would be passed to Italy and Yugoslavia when the RAF disposed of them. In exchange for the return of what the US estimated would be at least 370 Sabres, the RAF hoped for 350 Hunters, although the US government had to be advised that their estimations on 'returnable' aircraft were wrong. The US assumed that 90 Sabres remained unused in storage but the RAF estimated that by the end of 1954, there would be only 25 aircraft left in storage. Conversion onto the Hunter began late in 1955 and as each Sabre was withdrawn it was sent to a Maintenance Unit for overhaul. By the time of withdrawal many of the Sabres had been modified whilst in service, and the original wing with a leading-edge 'slat' device had been progressively replaced on many aircraft by a fixed wing of slightly greater span and chord, complete with a small wing fence. The aircraft that had yet to receive this modification were duly brought up to this standard after being phased out and slowly re-distributed to Italy and Yugoslavia. The final batch of aircraft delivered to Yugoslavia was not supplied as part of the original agreement, however, as relations between the US and Yugoslavia had deteriorated and MAP aid for that country was cancelled at the end of 1957. However, the aircraft that had yet to be delivered were paid for as an outright purchase from the US, and some 78 machines were delivered at a price of between $5,000 and $15,000 per aircraft. Some 302 aircraft were eventually refurbished and transferred to new operators and a further 52 Sabres were broken up as scrap. Despite having been overhauled at considerable expense, there was no further interest in them from Italy or Yugoslavia, and the US no longer had any need for them, and so the simplest means of disposing of the airframes was to simply write them off. Some were scrapped immediately although a few were still abandoned awaiting destruction even as late as 1973. The RAF's association with the Sabre was a remarkably short affair, but undoubtedly it was an enjoyable one. ❖

Twin-Seat Sabre

Initial design work on a twin-seat trainer derivative of the Sabre (the NA-204) began in April 1953, based on the F-86F-30 with a lengthened fuselage and with the wing moved forward by some eight inches to compensate for a shift in the aircraft's centre of gravity. Armament was deleted but slatted wings were retained. The USAF authorised the conversion of F-86F-30 serial number 52-5016 to two-seat configuration, re-designated as the TF-86F.
The type's maiden flight took place on 14 December 1953, with Ray Morris at the controls. Performance was similar to the F-86F although range was improved by some 300 miles, because of additional fuel capacity. Sadly, on 17 March 1954 (flight nine), NAA test pilot Joe Lynch lost control of the aircraft whilst attempting a slow roll after take-off, and the aircraft crashed, killing Lynch. The final F-86F-35 off the production line (53-1228) was modified to TF-86F configuration as a replacement. It was outwardly similar to the first TF-86F, but was armed with a pair of 0.50-in machine guns in the nose and equipped with external stored pylons. Additionally, a small ventral fin was added to the aft fuselage. The second TF-86F (53-1338) made its maiden flight on 5 August 1954 but during February 1955, the USAF announced that the TF-86F project would not be pursued, as plans were already under way to re-equip the USAF with the more advanced F-100 Super Sabre. The surviving TF-86 was assigned to Edwards AFB for use as a chase aircraft. *(Photos: Key Collection)*